WEL
LET'S EAT

BY

ROBIN DOUGLAS

Author of "16 to 21"

CASSELL
AND COMPANY LIMITED
LONDON, TORONTO, MELBOURNE
AND SYDNEY

First Published . . . *1933*

PRINTED IN GREAT BRITAIN

WHY I WROTE IT

It would be fun to start off with a long and serious discourse on the whys and wherefores of this book. At least, fun to write : maybe not to read. It is my intention, however, to forestall that question, " How on earth did you come to write on such a subject ? " Also, there is a certain malicious streak in me which delights in making other people raise their eyebrows. Why should they ? Well, it is rather an undertaking to set up oneself as a gastronomic guide to London. But I do, indeed, consider myself to be a superlatively good guide ; have had to make myself one in self-defence—for, during my more or less purposeless meanderings hither and yon, I have been asked so frequently :

" Tell me, where's a good place to eat in London ? "

There now. What a question.

It has been put to me by Americans in Paris ; Venetians in New York ; Austrians in Rome ; in fact, people of all nationalities in all countries additional to their own. People beset with the desire to go places, do things, see people and—eat.

Other emotions and desires are ephemeral, evanescent—so I have been informed. Eating, however—and by that let it be understood that drinking is also included—is a form of pleasurable dalliance which can be indulged again and again. Not so some certain other pursuits. Eating can be a bore, too ; such a bore. It is the desire to escape the bogy of boredom that makes sensible folk—like you, and you, and you —seek novelty in respect of food and all that is implied by that word.

Where's a good place to eat in London ?

Well, Greater London has an area of 693 square miles, which is no inconsiderable chunk of territory to be occupied by the dwellings and works of mankind : 7,476,170 units thereof, to be more or less precise.

It is a curious thing that all of these people, seven and a half millions of them nearly, have one thing in common : they eat. A deplorable habit formed in earliest childhood, and one that is wellnigh impossible to eradicate.

Whilst home cooking—by which I mean the preparation for consumption of foodstuffs in private houses as opposed to a restaurant's idea of home cooking—appears to satisfy the majority of Londoners for most of the year, yet there are occasions when even the most confirmed of arm-chair barnacles detaches itself ; heaves its carpet slippers or what not at the domestic cat or what-have-you and saunters forth in search of a nosebag containing something different. He calls this " going on a spree."

Restaurants cater to this group ; and right gladly.

Then there are the habitual " eaters-out." I'm one ;

for a variety of reasons. Singularly enough, the habituals actually prefer to eat in restaurants regularly, and indulge in home cooking by way of a change.

This group is the mainstay of restaurants.

Nor must it be forgotten that vast numbers of people visit London from all parts of the world. Folk who live more or less transiently in hotels, boarding-houses and apartments : flats, if you really prefer that designation. These people expect to be fed ; and patronize the city's restaurants with varying degrees of discrimination.

Among the visitors to London are those inveterate pioneers, explorers, Empire Builders—the Scots, who introduced to England the golden-hued haddock and —blessings upon them—whisky. Though they do eat salt with their porridge. . . .

Where's a good place to eat in London ?

That depends to a great extent upon what you want to eat. Maybe you have a yen for *canard à la presse* ; perhaps the thought of *capretto alla Piemontese* is what titillates your palate ; again, you may be feeling Teutonic, and with bulgy-neck noises demand to be supplied with *Kaiserschmarrn mit Erdberrn*. There are moments also, when there is nothing that appeals so much as a brown-speckled egg—boiled for three and a half minutes, please.

It depends on a great deal more than that just what you feel you would like to eat. For instance, one must take into consideration that not-so-unimportant item, the exchequer.

It depends on whether you wish to dress for dinner or prefer to be less formal. It depends on whether you like to eat at fox-trot tempo—or drink the wine of ancient Rome to a Wagnerian dirge.

Loath as I am to suggest such a thing, the choice of a place might even depend somewhat upon the wishes of your co-eater. For it is taken for granted that you do not intend to eat by yourself always. Such boorishness would be too relict of pre-cave days.

For many years I have ambled casually over various countries of Europe and America. Ostensibly to broaden my mind by educational travel. At least, that's a perfectly good excuse for poking my nose into out-of-the-way places in pursuit of interesting things to eat : interesting—and sometimes edifying —bottle to sample ; mayhap to empty.

Alas ! that I have to confess it. Most of my discoveries might have been made within a four-mile radius of Piccadilly Circus. A fact made apparent when it became out of the question for me to roam.

In a different way, it has been just as interesting and as much of an adventure exploring London. (Said he, as the grapes turned out to be slightly sour.) An inchoate city taking on colour from men and manners of all times and all places. In fact, a super mixed grill. Yes, a mixed grill. Even as that horrible dish is dominated by too much of one ingredient, so is London by the curse of uniform mediocrity. A pretty good slab of mediocrity at that.

There is a deadly sameness about the food in most London restaurants. As though it had all come from one central depot. It is difficult to find something tolerably good to eat that cannot be duplicated with mirror-like fidelity at that " other little restaurant just around the corner."

Discoveries can be made, however. A certain amount of wheedling—a little guile—a compliment or two, and, if necessary, a bellow like unto that of the bull of Bashan : these are the things that make restaurant proprietors remember those individualistic touches that make dishes different.

Yes : if you feel like it, and don't mind making scenes, do so : that treatment also has been known to get results from lethargic head waiters—sometimes.

Indeed, on occasions it takes a veritable typhoon of temperament to blast away the patina of uniformity and get at a restaurant's personality underneath.

It has been worth while ; this unmasking of London's restaurants.

Though I be condemned to a daily diet of dyspepsia tablets and water biscuits for many years to come, it has been fun collecting material for this book.

So come with me. Put on your best bib and tucker and let's wend our way on a quest more alluring than that of the Golden Fleece.

Let's eat.

COMMENTS
BY NORMAN DOUGLAS

Extracts from Letters written to
Robin Douglas

25th April 1932.

". . . I can't write a preface—haven't the time, as I am up to the neck in work (last year was my *worst* since long)—quite apart from the fact that I shouldn't know what to say. But if you send me the galley proofs of the book I'll go through it very carefully ; that would be better than the page proofs.

13th May 1932.

". . . 'Let's Eat' is a good idea.

14th June 1932.

". . . as to capretto or kid it is eaten at Easter because at that time of year it is in best condition. Nothing religious ; that particular nonsense is reserved for the lamb. . . ."

3rd Nov. 1932.

". . . Thanks for the noble Dedication. I must try to live up to that, but it will be difficult ! . . ."

He has kept the promise made in his letter of 25th April, 1932, and has gone through the galley proofs very carefully—pointing out errors of detail, punctuation, spelling and construction. For his practical and helpful advice and criticism I am really grateful—and have acted upon it.

On page 149 to my remark that *Hungary breeds fleet horses and strong wines* he suggests I add " and lovely women." I had overlooked that product of Hungary as it is not often exported—nor can I include the item in my text now in view of the sentence that would follow immediately after such addition.

On page 177 you will read, " *Last orders! Time, gentlemen, time! Come along now, please!* " My father says, " Here's your chance of 50 pages at that —— Dora." Not for me—let the Mayor of Deal attend to D.O.R.A.

On page 184 in the recipe for Risotto con Funghi mention is made of *grated cheese*. Apparently, this would be too ambiguous for the average reader— judging by the note alongside—" Better say Parmesan, eh? Else some . . . will grate Cheddar or Gorgonzola ! "

CORRIGENDA

Since writing this book :—

Eats Ltd. has changed hands, and I have no personal experience of it under its present ownership (*see* pp. 36-38).

Le Grill Caucasien at the Hotel Splendide is no more. Captain Vivien has transferred his Russian motif *en masse* to Kasbek in *Jermyn Street, W.1*.

Roy Fox is no longer at Monseigneur Restaurant. He is now *chef d'orchestre* at Kit Cat, whilst Lew Stone has taken over at the former place (*see* p. 155).

Here is something to add, by way of consolation—if you like German cooking, that is. Go to Schmidt's at 41 *Charlotte Street, W.1*, for the best and cheapest German food this side of the North Sea. Ask for Paul, my favourite waiter : he'll look after you.

WELL, LET'S EAT

GENNARO'S, 63, *New Compton Street.*

" Good-a evening ! How many you are, pleez ? "

" A nice flower, Madam ! Specially picked for you in Bordighera ! Fresh to-day ! "

" Lovely turkee—specialle toonight ! "

" 'O-o-ot pla-a-a-tes, Ja-a-ack ! "

" Piatti caldi-i-ah ! "

" Mind your ba-agks, pleez ! "

Such sentences as these together with similar less intelligible vocal expressions : snatches of warbled—I mean " garbled "—song from operatically-inclined waiters : pushing and shoving : pounding of flat feet on uncarpeted stairs : the unmusical crash of dozens of knives and forks cascading into wooden boxes : the clatter of thick crockery : these are the component parts of that anthem of cacophony that signifies but one thing—the narrow entrance to Gennaro's Restaurant, in New Compton Street.

This noise business is nothing but a racket : stupendous—incredible—magnificent—but a racket none the less : in the American sense of the word. Gennaro's, astute Italians that they are, realized that people wanted a restaurant that would approximate to mental pictures of eating-places in the " sunny laughing South." Gennaro's gave the public what it wanted.

Gave it with both hands ; openly and freely gave the public the noisiest and showiest Italian restaurant, north, south, east and west of Naples. In which city there is none noisier—since Mussolini did away with the open-air street kitchens.

Bona fide Neapolitans accustomed to stridency are awe-struck by the din : awe-struck, dazed and defeated by it.

The smiles, smirks, bows and " a flower for the lady " have won for Gennaro's an unwavering popularity with the gentler sex. Gennaro's restaurant is " sitting pretty."

King Bomba, a neighbouring Italian produce merchant and long-time customer of this restaurant, has lost his voice. I insist that this was caused by him trying to make himself heard through the din raised by ham-handed, ham-footed waiters.

From the foregoing it would seem that I infer Gennaro's to be a noisy place. Well, it is. And the more it expands the more noise there is. And that brings more customers, so that it expands yet again, and that . . . oh dear ! Where will it stop ?

Now I used to know the place in its very early days : some twenty years ago. That was when the restaurant consisted of one room only, and a cubbyhole. On the ground floor right, as you go into the place. Now the place has spread laterally and perpendicularly out of all recognition—since the days when Gennaro would make a big ginger cat jump through his locked hands, for my amusement and edification. The cat disappeared. . . .

Every room of this restaurant is decorated in a different style. Rather bewildering ; but it gives the diner a wide choice of surroundings. Personally, I plump for the room at the top : the one called the Green Room : and would like it even better were the lighting more subdued. There are other reasons why I would recommend this particular room. One is that although there is plenty of bustle, yet there is also an atmosphere of soft green and red restfulness, induced by the decorations, militating against the noise of downstairs. The second reason is, Achille the head waiter. He is an old friend of mine : has tended to my wants since I was " knee high to a grasshopper." And that's a long time. He is a sympathetic kindly soul, and seems to have retained his poise and balance despite the startling exhibitions of showmanship displayed by other members of the Gennaro staff. Yes : I commend you to Achille's care—certain that he will look after you right well.

Like the majority of Italian restaurants in London, Gennaro's has no licence ; something to do with our inane laws, I believe. The result is that in addition to a swarm of cashiers, hat-check girls, waiters, plate-and-dish carriers, there is a host of minor fry, wearing long white aprons : these are the wine boys whose

3   B

job it is to scuttle to the public-house on the corner and bring in wine, spirits and mere beer as ordered.

It is a nuisance—this wine-boy business. Barely are you in your chair, when a microbe standing about a yard high plunks the wine list under your nose. Between you and me, what is there worth drinking after the bottle has been swung airily by the neck all the way from the pub on the corner ? Nothing—excepting ice water, and you can get that gratis from Gennaro's. Still, these wine boys have to justify their existence, I suppose. So, if you feel like drinking wine, order some reputable brand such as Orvieto ; or Albano—alleged to come from Rome. Don't forget this item by the way : there is no such thing as real Capri wine : Capri-type, maybe : but not real Capri. There's not enough produced on that island to satisfy the inhabitants thereof : certainly there's no thought of exporting any for London people to drink. Brolio of the year 1927 is a good Chianti—if you can get it.

Coming now to that important matter of food, there is somewhat of a problem confronting me. There is the ubiquitous *scaloppino milanese* which one can get from Nova Zembla to Penguin Island. There is the equally well-known *crême caramel* : Italy's stand-by in the dessert section. There is every other concoction known both to yourself and all Italian restaurateurs. In addition to these things—did I forget to mention

4

our old friend " *vol-au-vent Toulouse* " ?—this restaurant caters to its public inasmuch as it presents three specialities each day and every day of the week ; by which I mean different specialities, of course. Here they are, for your edification : I do not intend to translate the Italian : after all, that is the waiter's job.

Monday.	maccheroni au gratin ossobuco alla milanese entrecote alla pizzaiolo.
Tuesday.	risotto con fegatini di pollo ris de veau en cocotte granadine di vitello.
Wednesday.	homard à l'Américaine cannelloni alla siciliana salti in bocca al risotto.
Thursday.	maccheroni stufati siciliana rollatini de vitello côte de veau milanaise.
Friday.	bouillabaisse all' Italiana ravioli ai spinaci cervelle alla parmigiana.
Saturday.	lasagne alla Mussolini trippa alla genovese stracotto di bue.
Sunday.	manzo e pollo puchero arrostini annegati braciole napolitane.

All those things are in the nature of entrées you'll

notice. At least, they are all savoury. Now, in the way of desserts, this restaurant does rather better than the average Italian place. Pancakes, fruit salad, sticky cream-and-rum-soaked cake, coupe Jacques and the like, go without saying. I would call to your notice, for trial at least once, that latest effort of Gennaro's. A species of open fruit tart : cherries, figs, apples, plums and I know not what others besides, all smothered in cream. What a concoction. Try it once, anyway ; in the pioneer spirit of exploration. I've had to, so that I could tell you about it.

An attempt to nail either of the brother proprietors to say what they considered to be the real specialities of their restaurant was a hopeless task.

A shrug of the shoulders : waving of plump hands : " Oh ! bud you see, we 'ave specialitays everee day ! "

Of course ! But with all the goodwill in the world, it was not my intention to go into the details of preparation of twenty-one dishes. Not likely. So, by dint of much persuasion, we finally selected the following as being most indigenous to the place.

Trippa alla Genovese (for four persons).

Ingredients. 1 section garlic ; 1 carrot ; Spanish onion ; 2 tomatoes ; 2 oz. butter ; 2 oz. olive oil ; 1 lb. tripe ; herbs ; parsley ; basilic ; bay leaf ; celery leaf ; leek.

Put oil and butter with onion cut up in slices, and

6

section of garlic finely chopped into casserole and cook to a golden brown. Add 1 dessert-spoon of flour and mix well. Add tripe, which should be cut in small pieces—tomatoes finely chopped—1 pint of stock and season to taste. Tie carrot, leek and celery leaf in a bunch and put in casserole. Cook slowly for 1¼ hours. Before serving hot, add basilic, parsley and bay leaf which have been finely chopped. Take out bunch of vegetables.

Bouillabaisse all' Italiana (for four persons).

Ingredients. 2 live lobsters about ¾ lb. each ; 4 tomatoes ; carrot ; Spanish onion ; 2 oz. butter ; 2 oz. olive oil.

Cut up vegetables finely and lobsters in small pieces—place with oil and butter in a sauté pan, cook over quick fire until brown. Add chopped tomatoes, 2½ pints of fish stock and season to taste. Cook twenty-five to thirty minutes. Then add 1 lb. mixed fish (eels—mussels—mackerel—whiting—gun-net—sole—turbot) cut in pieces and cook for fifteen minutes. Serve hot on silver dish, garnishing with chopped parsley and small pieces of bread which have been fried in a little oil.

Now, that first dish is tripe—I mean its chief ingredient is tripe. A word synonymous in my personal lexicography with " uneatable." Admittedly, it's an unjustifiable prejudice—but there it is. I don't like tripe, even when served " alla Genovese." I wouldn't care if all the Italian cities lent the combined weight of their names to the dish. It's made of tripe. And for me there's an end on't. Other people like it. All right. They can have it. My share too.

The bouillabaisse I suspect of being a cousin to that obtainable in sailors' eating dives on the waterfront of Marseilles. Though I affirm unhesitatingly that Gennaro's version is very much better bred : more educated : rayfeened. The genuine *zuppa da pesce* such as one attempts to eat in Genoa or Spezia is a thing of disillusion. Weird, prehistoric sea beasties that are all anatomy—and mighty little edible on it—swimming disconsolately in garlicky, lukewarm water with a few stale crusts therein. No, no. Gennaro's bouillabaisse is definitely eatable. The liquid part is enriched, thickened and coloured by the tomato ; there are pieces of fish perfectly recognizable and entirely eatable, whilst the baked toast crusts are authentic. For half an hour's fun in spluttering over fish bones ; beating toast crusts in gravy and having a deal of work generally, I suggest the bouillabaisse. Not before going to a theatre, however : for there is garlic in this dish : dear me, yes ! Just a soupçon of it, but it's enough.

If you like to eat spaghetti occasionally—and if you don't, you have no business visiting Italian restaurants

—try *spaghetti espressissimi alla marinara*. That too has just the ghost of a whiff of garlic in the sauce. It's worth while, however.

A small item that has always amazed me, is the tremendous display of really excellent fresh fruits here. Gennaro's has as good a selection as any crackerjack hotel in London. It is an item that commends itself to me particularly.

Yes : if you go upstairs and put yourself in the hands of Achille : or, if you must eat downstairs, if you can shut your ears to the noise : if you can appreciate with the right spirit the flamboyancy of the decorations : if you can convince the waiter that you are not in a hurry to catch a train and do not wish to be hustled through your meal ; then it is possible to eat really well at Gennaro's. It's worth while, too.

Some day, I expect the proprietors will invite me to have " dinner on the house." Why ? Well, I have been a good patron of theirs for twenty years. That last sentence should be enough to tell you that this restaurant is far from expensive. Besides, think of all the display and " a flower for the lady " that you get for your money !

So au revoir to Gennaro's—the most cheerful Italian restaurant in London.

Come, then, with me on a personally-conducted whirlwind tour of some more of London's Italian res-

taurants ! These are chiefly to be found in that un-
lovely district of Soho. No amount of history : no
efforts of rhetoric and no verbal whitewashing will ever
change my opinion of Soho : it's a dingy tangle of
slatternly streets, comprised for the most part of drab,
dreary and unkempt little houses. Yet it is the London nesting place of cheap restaurants : for the most
part of Italian genre.

Farther along New Compton Street, on the next
corner in fact, we come to *Tony's*. (That name is
shared by at least fifteen thousand of New York's
speakeasies. Of no importance, or significance, however.) This place is quieter, more sedate, less flamboyant
than its boisterous neighbour we have been discussing.
Thus there is a definite niche in the scheme of life
for such a place as Tony's. The mood for reason-
ably-good, reasonably-priced Italian food in peaceful
surroundings . . . with no bombastic pretensions :
that's where this restaurant comes into its own.

It is smaller, too. Which is no fault, to my way
of thinking. Though the menu may not be so varied
as Gennaro's, yet what there is to eat is always well
prepared, well cooked and decently served. The
decorations are very nearly right : that is, you almost
don't notice them. Unfortunately they do just catch
your eye, and so the mischief is done.

Tony's has no dominating human personality. Some
people may deplore that. I don't. It's pleasant to

relax here and be some one of a certain—though momentary—importance to the waiter. He is not working hard to play up to a created atmosphere and reputation.

As for wine . . . the same old " pub on the corner " business has to be gone through ; which is usual in Soho, however.

The food, whilst not being calculated to set the pulses leaping, is of a definitely high standard.

Why not try a perfectly straightforward escaloppe of veal, cooked slowly in a sauce to which white wine has been added ? On top of the little piece of veal, there should be a squadron of very young mushrooms.

Incidentally, the minestrone here is really excellent. Minestrone ? That filling-up vegetable *pôt au feu* of Italy ? Yes : and why not ?

From personal experience, I know these two things to be good and can commend them to your attention.

Enough of Tony's. Pleasant and amiable though it would be to loiter awhile, and drink another strega or so with the young proprietor, we must hurry along.

Poke our noses into those two quite simple restaurants, the *Mars* in Frith Street and the *Fava* in Greek Street.

Nobody's feelings will be hurt if I say that these places are of the bourgeois order. They have their appointed destinies to fulfil ; and there are times aplenty when my purse being unusually slender, such little places have a strong appeal for me.

The clientèle of such places is amusing also, however. Nondescript writers, artists and other pursuers of the arts. Those rather paunchy gentlemen who lay fingers on the sides of noses and say " I know a little place in Soho." One or two pretty girls ; and always a leavening of the local Italian population. Which latter can be regarded as a good omen. It's a guarantee of genuine value for money.

Having set out to be truthful in the recounting of these peregrinations, it pains me to notice that the *Villa Villa Restaurant* in Gerrard Street has changed considerably since those days when I was a fairly frequent patron. It has become table d'hôte and à la carte : with the balance heavily on the side of the former. The general run of table d'hôte meals are anathema to me. Still, for a cheap and really good value-for-money Italian table d'hôte this restaurant has its uses. After all, I'm not the only person in the world. . . .

Corti's is a tiny eating-place at the Wardour Street end of Old Compton Street. I am curious to know if, after a visit there, you carry away impressions similar to mine own. Namely, glistening white paintwork and pink-shaded lights. From which I deduce perfectly logically that the food must be perfectly satisfactory ; the prices I know are more than reasonable : had they not been, I should be bewailing the cost loud and long. Wait a moment, though ! I remember eating a particularly tender veal cutlet with some *Tagliatelli Bolognese* and deciding it was good. That's right. Nor can I do otherwise than suggest you eat the same when visiting this small place.

TROCADERO "SHORT" BAR.

As most habitués know perfectly well, there is a Jamaican cocktail shaker at the Trocadero "Short" Bar. Some may not be aware of his existence owing to the fact that they make this place their last port of call in a convivial evening. This negro is a show-man, inasmuch as he flings the bottles into the air, and manipulates the shaker with one peculiar flick of the wrist. All his work is showy : that's what the customers like apparently, and they pay for it.

Myself, I prefer more care and deliberation to be expended upon the correct preparation of something intended to be put inside me. Anyway, cocktails as such have very little interest for me : very little, or, shall we say, not so much as other drinks have ?

There is another bartender in addition to our West Indian friend—and I mean the much-travelled man with the sleek black hair brushed straight back.

For him I entertain a definite weakness ; bred of the fact that he knows the constituent parts of that excellent drink, Whisky Sour. Nor does he make the mistake committed by a bartender in a certain well-known Strand hostelry, who used Scotch whisky : the only brand to use is Canadian Club—for a real Whisky

Sour relies on that insidious, smoky, rye flavour for its excellence.

That's where the " Short " Bar expert betrays his knowledge. Without faltering, he picks out the Canadian Club when asked for Whisky Sour.

My only regret is, that he measures it out with that peculiarly microscopic thimble which is part of every London drinking-place. Were I a rich man, it would be a pleasure to invite all those responsible for that wretched thimble measure to come to a New York speakeasy and see the way a bartender there pours out whisky with a lavish hand : not drop by drop, as though it were more precious than radium.

Of course, there are a multitude of other things to drink at the " Short " Bar. Cocktails large and small : mere beer and ale ; both dark and pale : sherries, ports, liqueurs and so forth. For me, however, there is but that one drink : long, cool, refreshing, subtle and insinuating. A comforting, gratitude-engendering drink : a pleasure-to-see-it-being-made drink : Whisky Sour. The ideal drink to chase a Whisky Sour is another Whisky Sour, followed by yet another.

Three is really all one should have to provoke that golden glow . . . to stimulate that feeling of well-being toward our fellow-men . . . of course, if you insist upon having a fourth, who am I to say you nay ?

Very well, then.

So be it.

And another after that because odd numbers are lucky . . . you say it's too late to go to dinner and a show ? Cut out the show and postpone dinner for another half-hour or so . . . that gives time for just two more . . . and after that, what do we care ?

BLUE COCKATOO, *Cheyne Walk, Chelsea.*

A time there was when I lived in Chelsea, and amused and occupied myself in the way that Chelsea-ites do ; or did, rather. For things are " not what they used to be in the good old days."

During that superlatively adolescent period of intense writing, I patronized Chelsea's restaurants. In the days when I didn't care what I ate ! What a confession. Still, it was true.

Amongst those places honoured by my presence and cash-patronage was the Blue Cockatoo in Cheyne Walk. What an ideal situation. Overlooking the river and across to Battersea Park : all around, houses of personality inhabited by people of none. Immediately in front, the Chelsea Embankment Gardens; a strip nearly six yards wide devoted to weary trees and discouraged grass. Slightly to the left front that completely unimportant suspension bridge named after Albert the Good.

With such surroundings, the Blue Cockatoo should have been either exceedingly good, or else exceedingly Chelseafied. I suggest you make your own decision after trying the place.

There is no doubt about it : the Blue Cockatoo has a definite personality all its own. The kind of a personality that sighs graciously with a dignified acquiescence in the new order of things. The house is old and must be full of ghosts : but they are pleasant, friendly ghosts who bid you welcome—and as you sit awhile, charm away your thoughts to those romantic colourful days when gallants strolled along the riverside, doffing plumed hats to fair ladies. An intermittent patronage extending over a period of nine years has been my experience of this restaurant : never once has the Blue Cockatoo failed to cast its spell over me.

Luncheon, though perfectly satisfactory, is not my time of day for going thither. Teatime is the right hour : and tea is the meal I commend without reservations.

Ask Hetty, the waitress, if you can have home-made scones and strawberry jam.

" Don't make scones here," she will tell you. " Only got plum jam."

So order buttered toast and China tea.

" No China tea," says Hetty.

So resign yourself to your fate. For Hetty, frail wisp of a thing that she is, rules the roost here. In ten minutes she returns and places before you home-made scones, China tea, and strawberry jam. But then that's Hetty all over, you see. She has a phobia against admitting that customers can have what they

16

want. She'd hate it to be thought that she will bully the cook into making scones right away. Sure enough, there are times when she won't : those are the occasions when Hetty stands silently by your table, while you give your order. If she doesn't say a word, it means you'll get brought to you whatever is the least trouble for Hetty. Yet everyone loves her—and she has a warm corner in her heart for her " regulars."

Upstairs there is a window seat at the front end of the room. Here it is more than pleasant to sit for a summer hour drinking tea and watching the traffic swishing along the Embankment. Any bickering downstairs is muffled : there are no ghosts at all in this room ; only an atmosphere of peaceful content. Perhaps you will be visited by Anne and Tony : those attractive children of the proprietress : these two are growing up at a most alarming rate.

There is no electric light at the Blue Cockatoo, or was not up to my last visit there. So one dines in the pleasant mellow glow of candles : which engenders that feeling of peace and well-being. Candlelight does a great deal towards softening the harsh influences of daily toil and strife.

STONE'S CHOP HOUSE, 32, *Panton Street*, *W*.1.

Apparently, this place was famous in those good old days that belong to the age of myths ; namely, any time not of the present generation.

There is nothing particularly prepossessing about the outside of Stone's to catch your eye. In truth, it is a dingy-looking little place, apparently trying to escape attention. Inside the entrance passage, and it really is no more than a passage, it is just as dark and dingy-looking. Well, what does that matter? People, sensible people that is, don't go to Stone's to eat the panelled walls. They go to eat steaks and chops and such like goodly English fare.

Before going farther I'd like to call your attention to a remarkable item. All the very best chop houses in London have one thing in common: they are all long established. I used to think that the grilling of a chop or a steak was something that could only be done in a fireplace not less than a hundred years old. Now I've discovered why such places are old; and I'll let you into the secret, too.

The reason why chop houses are old is as follows. Nearly all of them pride themselves on serving an excellent entrée called steak-and-kidney pudding; at some places a few odd mushrooms are included; maybe a lark or two; or some oysters. These steak-and-kidney puddings take the very deuce of a long time to cook to be really right; and that is why chop houses are all so old: they have been forced to renew their ninety-nine year leases frequently simply because the original steak-and-kidney pudding was not cooked.

Another thing. Let me correct myself before

Charles, the head waiter of Stone's, throws me into the stockpot. There is no such thing as an " entrée " at this place ; such dishes are termed " removes." Why ? I don't know ; but there it is.

Perhaps when Charles has been rather longer with Stone's he may be able to explain quite a lot of things to me. But then, after all, he has only been there thirty-seven years. Barely time for a really genuine English waiter to take off his coat and begin work. As a young American lady of the variety stage re-marked, Charles looks " real cute " in his Tudor costume. This is a white shirt, white apron, brown knickerbockers and scarlet waistcoat. I wonder if " cute " is quite the right word to apply to Charles ? Perhaps not.

On the Bill of Fare—which means " menu " to you, O Ye of Little Learning—the first thing we see is that Stone's was established in 1770. Just 163 years ; and that, I think, must be time enough for the first batch of steak-and-kidney puddings to be cooked.

Let's eat.

If I poked fun at things a little way back, I am genuinely repentant now. This is not a steak-and-kidney pudding ; it is a poem of which every bit is perfect. The slow cooking makes the steak absorb some of the kidney's characteristics and vice versa ; and in a calm dreamy way they go on swapping essences all through the long time of cooking. So that when you get the finished pudding it is, as I have said, perfect. It melts in the mouth, quite literally.

The correct thing after this is a " follow " of toasted cheese, and the liquid is beer or ale ; or half and half ; or lager. But for mercy's sake, don't get all Frenchified and ask for a bottle of Chablis ; Charles is a valued friend to thousands, and such an order would give him nervous prostration. The alcoholic product of malt and hops is the thing. In fact if you like it, I strongly advise Bass's Number 1. More alcoholic content. . . .

Other specialities of Stone's are grilled Scotch salmon when in season ; and—of all things !—curried chicken and rice.

I would call your attention to the eatables listed " From the Grill." First, there is Chop ; then comes Chump Chop. Later down the list is Mutton Cutlets (2). And they all cost 1s. 8d. a time. Ye gods, though ; what chops they are ! It seems they must have been carved from mastodonic creatures ; yet they are as tender as . . . as tender as . . . well, they are very tender indeed !

There are all manner of sporting prints and the like on the walls to engage your attention if you feel that way inclined ; but the purpose of Stone's is to provide large helpings of food at very reasonable prices ; food that is excellently cooked in the best English way—which, alas, is becoming relegated to the regions of tradition ; but not at Stone's.

A final hint to you.

When you have your toasted cheese it is as well to remember that Stone's is famous for making an excellent punch ; order some and drink it with your " follow." Ha ! Got the name right that time, eh, Charles ?

RISTORANTE DEL COMMERCIO, 65, *Frith Street*, *W*.1.

Occasionally it is fun for the mind, and a relief to the digestive organs, to pay a quiet visit to an eating place of little or no pretensions. A restaurant that does not " put on dog " as it is termed in certain New York circles.

Such a place is the Ristorante del Commercio at 65, Frith Street, in Soho. In fact, so unassuming is this place that it is but fairly recently the bay trees in tubs have been put by the front door. The restaurant has an inconspicuous signboard, more or less illuminated in the evening.

It would be singularly easy to overlook this restaurant entirely—unless you knew of it. My painter friend, Adolf Birkenruth, first took me to the Commercio. Since then, I have taken many people there. That's the way this place builds up a clientèle.

Mr. Prevedini is the proprietor. A nice, simple, kindly soul with a large gold coin on his watch chain. His wife and charming daughter make up the ménage.

You are greeted warmly on entering ; you sit where you like—if your favourite table happens to be free ; you hang up your own coat on a hook ; and Teresa, the little waitress, cuts off a few pieces of bread from the yard-long loaf.

What will you have ?

A choice of a dozen hors-d'œuvre at eightpence : minestrone soup at fourpence ; *spaghetti alla bolognese* at ninepence ? Or perhaps a " nize grabèfru' " at sixpence ?

Sole, fried, meunière or Colbert is two shillings. That is the highest-priced item on the menu. There is a choice of rather less than a dozen entrées at one-and-eight. Four sweets at sixpence a time ; the usual cheese, fruit and coffee details.

There may be three copies of the menu ; written by Signorina Prevedini ; possibly only two copies. The wine list is, I believe, engraven on the tablets of memory of the girl who acts as Mercury.

In the room upstairs are two prints of patriotic Italian pictures. The rest of the decorations consists of white-painted walls, relieved here and there by colourful advertisements. Oh yes ; there are sure to be flowers on the tables.

The habitués ? A few would-be highbrows discussing such things as art, the theatre, inferiority complexes : why must the most empty-headed young man always have the loudest voice ? Local Italians—

cronies of *famiglia* Prevedini. A few wise men of the East—and West—who seek simple, straightforward cooking.

Orders are shouted through a hatchway; when ready, the plates are pushed through that same orifice. Your bill is made out on a scrap of paper with a pencil borrowed—from you, in all probability.

Vegetables don't figure on the menu at all. The appropriate potatoes and so forth are served with your order, as a matter of course.

No flim-flamming; no gewgaws. Just honest, good food; cooked properly and served nicely. The prices, as already mentioned, are such as commend themselves to all—save the completely destitute.

I asked, what were the specialities.

"The specialities? Oh, I don't know . . . well, we have spaghetti, fritto misto, cotelette milanesi and zambaglione."

The ordinary everyday fare. Having just eaten *fegato venezia*, my next question was anent the preparation of this dish.

"Oh! That's very easy! Cut up liver into little thin pieces. And an onion, too. Fry them together in butter. When nearly cooked, add a little white wine. That's all."

Yes. That's all. Very easy. And how good it was. Zambaglione is Italy's major contribution to the world's list of desserts. A much-beaten yolk of egg to

23

which marsala and sugar are added ; served hot in a glass. That's not so easy to get right, as it is more than likely that the finished product may be lumpy ; therefore quite hopeless. A good zambaglione is a thing to cherish in your memory.

Now I have got a howl to make. I hope the good Signor Prevedini will make a note of it, and seek a remedy for the complaint. Why, oh why is it impossible to get a cup of coffee in an Italian restaurant ? I mean coffee that tastes as that beverage should ? The people of Italy can mix coffee in more varied flavours than that of any other country on the face of the earth. It's an inherent, national disability on the part of Italians. A pity.

Nevertheless, in spite of that, Ristorante Commercio will see me again and again and again. It's a haven of peace, where one eats decently and oh ! so cheaply.

SOHO CAFÉ BARS.

One approaches these places in the spirit of adventure. Like the majority of such adventures, the mystery part fizzles out rapidly ; because there is no mystery attaching to a Soho café bar.

They are not ideal haunts for ladies of gentle nurture, nevertheless ; inasmuch as these café bars cater for the honest labouring classes. In the case of a good many of these patrons neither " honest " nor " labouring " applies.

After which preamble, be it noted that these few paragraphs concern men only ; in fact, the film censor would award " A " certificate, and not " U " to this, my commentary on such a distinctive feature of Soho.

A café bar is exactly what is implied by the name. A counter-bar being the main article of furniture with high stools for customers ; sometimes, in the more pretentious places, there may be a rickety table or two. Only if space permits.

Perched on these stools at all hours of the day for as long as the café is open, are those gentlemen who toil not, neither do they spin. Yet Solomon in all his glory could not have been so flashily dressed as some of these coffee-drinking idlers.

Other customers there are. A few quiet and studious elderly men reading Italian, French or German newspapers. Some others, who are only just not destitute ; possessing the necessary coppers to buy coffee and drink it in comparative comfort—what time they rest their weary behinds.

One or two sisters of joy : ladies of easy virtue : prostitutes of the cheaper, rougher type—who would consider even one of those near-destitutes in the light of " trade," for the sake of a shilling or so.

Although the mainstay of the café bar's business is the purveying of coffee, yet tea and cocoa can be bought also. Cakes too : ye gods ! what cakes. One needs the mentality of a magpie to appreciate the gaudiness of these comestibles; the digestion of an ostrich to eat one without experiencing ill-effects. What may prove surprising is the ham rolls on sale at these establishments. Notably in the case of *Au Chat Noir*—a café bar in Old Compton Street. The ham rolls at this place are really good. Heaven knows why they should be.

Certain café bars sell cigarettes of all nationalities; papers also. A few stock Toscani: those strong and crinkly-shaped Italian cigars, which in Italy cost about a ha'penny each: in London, fivepence; thanks to those responsible for protective tariffs.

Those tawdry, too-smartly tailored men who sit at the counter, now. What is it that impels them to waste so much of the day thusly? How is it that, having no work apparently, they are able to dress in a pseudo-fashionable, fake-good manner? Maybe they are all night-workers. Perhaps they make a living through backing horses or through other people backing horses—that would seem more possible.

It is unlikely that I shall ever learn the truth of these drab, butterfly youths of Soho. They and their *modus operandi* do not interest me sufficiently to stimulate me to more pertinent investigation. To blazes with their lewd jokes, and ribald remarks to the girl who serves them with coffee—wearily and mechanically defending her person from the touch of their bestial, searching hands . . . these creatures seeking cheap

26

thrills at the expense of a down-trodden, underpaid serving girl.

Don't run away with the idea that this sort of thing is a perpetual side-show at the café bars. It occurs only at one or two of the very lowest and scruffiest. The majority of these places are quiet, orderly and well-conducted ; with no more excitement than that afforded by a non-paying customer being frog-marched on to the pavement.

Again referring to Au Chat Noir (being a place I frequented often). The coffee here is good also : of Continental type : Switzerland, I think it is, that brews coffee of the same flavour as that found in here. Certainly, it is not that nauseous concoction the Italians like—a compound of ground chicory root and cab-horse hooves.

Chess and dominoes are played by the hour, by the well-behaved regular patrons of such places. Many a game of chess I've played with a Greek hairdresser in a Frith Street café bar.

These places have their uses : they have their devotees. My days of such are over ; and except for an experimental excursion, I cannot see you, and you, and you becoming café bar lounge lizards.

MARTINEZ, *Spanish Restaurant*, 25, *Swallow Street*, *W*.1.

Should you wake up from a sound sleep with the click of castanets and the soft, melodious strumming of guitars in your dream-ears, then I can supply the reason for your sudden awakening.

You have been dining at Martinez's. You have been sitting in the Andalusian Patio. You have been going gay in an Iberian manner.

That Andalusian Patio is the dining-room. Disregarding the appurtenances of a public restaurant, it is very much like the real thing in Spain. In that same Patio is even a fountain, the gentle splash and drip-drip of whose waters inspire many thoughts of cool, sun- and shade-dappled courtyards.

The King of Spain and his sons have honoured Martinez with their patronage. Segovia too ; likewise Augustus John. Jacob Epstein has eaten here. De Falla and Padilla, representing the world of music, have dined at the Spanish Restaurant. These are but a few of the many distinguished, discerning and discriminating people who have been to this place.

" Customers are respectfully informed that no cheques can be accepted." That item on the menu fairly leaps at you from the surrounding print. I know of no other good restaurant in London where such a piece of information is written on the menu : right underneath Saturday's specialities.

In hard-boiled dives and speakeasies I've seen a card stuck up announcing " No credit : no checks." Never did I expect to find a house of Martinez's fame having to state the fact baldly in type.

Unfortunate Martinez's Restaurant! How many stumer cheques they must have had to accept, compelling them to take such a step. Seeing the notice makes one itch to pay by cheque. . . . Without doubt, there must be excellent justification for the management's display of the " no cheques " notice : it is couched in singularly polite terms, which remove the sting.

For some reason or other, this place has a reputation for being expensive. Which is absurd, for it is extremely reasonable in price : and the food is good. Indeed, it is superlatively good. Martinez would not bear a Royal Warrant from his Majesty the King of Spain were the food other than excellent. You may be sure of that.

There are certain daily specialities listed on the menu. If you can read Spanish, then you are among the blessed few. For those numerous others the waiters will translate anything into any language. And these are special dishes which can be ordered any day of the week : dishes which take from ten to twenty-five minutes to cook.

These are the things especially recommended to you. Goodness me! You've come to a Spanish restaurant and eat Spanish food you Spanish well will, whether you Spanish well like it or not!

Of course if you insist upon it, you can have a table d'hôte luncheon for three shillings and a table d'hôte dinner for four-and-six. Being menus which do "not include any Spanish dishes." Rather naïve.

Should you refuse to begin your meal with a glass of sherry you will insult irrevocably three people : the waiter, the manager and myself. Especially do I commend that pale, dry sherry with the bouquet and flavour of nuts. There're not many places can boast of a sherry of such amiable mellowness. Don't have more than two glasses—for, after all, there are the other wines of Spain to be considered.

For instance. There is a Rioja Red wine under the shipper's name of Marques Murrietta, which is excellent and only seven-and-six a bottle. A Rioja White at five-and-six, for which I don't much care, and other Spanish wines from four shillings a bottle.

If you prefer it, you can drink whisky and soda or ginger beer. If you do, then it is certain that you have forgotten the maxim of "when in Rome," etc.

Here are the recipes for a typical Spanish luncheon. No : I do not know what the names of the dishes are when translated :

Arroz à la Valenciana (four persons).

In a frying-pan place some oil, when hot add a whole chicken, cut in about eight pieces, wait till brown and add some finely cut onions and pimentoes, also a suspicion of garlic and small pieces of ham or pork. When this preparation is cooked add four coffee-cupfuls of rice, mix the whole well and add nine coffee-cups of stock, then some green peas, French beans and a few mussels ; boil the whole preparation, adding a pinch of saffron and salt, stir the lot until the spoon stands almost erect in the centre. You can finish same in the oven.

Bunuelos à la Sevillana.

One pound of flour, one pint of milk and eight eggs are the only ingredients necessary to make this delicious sweet. Boil the milk and mix the flour well, then place over the fire again for half a minute, remove and then add one egg at a time.

Sabrosos Pradera.

A piece of cheese (Petit Gruyère) cut in the middle ; soak same in milk for ten minutes, then dip it in breadcrumbs, and in beating eggs and in breadcrumbs again, add a little cayenne or paprika, flattened with a knife to form a firm crust. Put in a frying-pan good olive oil and when hot fry same for two minutes, when it will be brown and crusty. Serve hot.

Now, that first dish is a very intricate risotto. Read the recipe again and you will see that there are at least twelve different things that go into the making of it. A portion of it at Martinez's takes twenty-five minutes to prepare and costs three shillings and sixpence. If you intend to eat it, go into starvation training for a week beforehand, as the proprietors are not niggardly with the portions.

The second recipe is a dessert. To the majority of people, it is a dessert for which one has to acquire a taste.

The third is a savoury. This is the thing at the sight of which all good Spaniards seize guitars and play The Bolero for all they are worth. This is the only dish that can lure a bullfighter from the arena. This is the dish . . . well, what I'm getting at, and trying to make you understand, is, that it's excellent. Have some. The fact that it has been dipped " in beating eggs " should persuade you to try it once.

Most definitely Martinez's is excellent. As a restaurant of the best Spanish kind it is unique in London; and such good wine and at such reasonable prices.

SANDY'S SANDWICH BAR, *Oxenden Street, W.1.*

A bar where they serve sandwiches; also coffee and tea, and, I believe, soft drinks.

It is noteworthy that the majority of people regard all sandwich bars with disfavour. A primary reason for this disfavour being that they supply the wrong kind of food: wrong, inasmuch as it is too easily masticated and not easily digested. A second reason being, that the prices charged are usually quite outrageous; and out of all proportion to the value of the food and service. A third reason being, that a sandwich bar is invariably a detestably uncomfortable place : generally grimy, and usually smelly. A fourth reason being, the clientèle.

These reasons, however, are usually put forward by people who feel grouchy toward any form of quick service places. Innovation of any kind is hailed as omen of doom by this type of Diehard. Actually, sandwich bars fill a real need. Take Sandy's Sandwich Bar in Oxenden Street ; a grubby and unpleasant thoroughfare which is, as you may know, close to the Haymarket and parallel with it.

It is the proud boast of this place—founded by one Kenelm Foss quondam Thespian—that they have a list of one hundred and twenty varieties of sandwiches : of which the daily menu offers sixty. That may be the case and probably is ; not having seen their list, I must accept the statement at its face value.

Another proud boast of Sandy's is that all the ingredients of their sandwiches are Empire products. They have a large pictorial map of the world showing the place of origin of each thing. One thing you will not discover on the map : and that is margarine.

A third proud boast is the coffee served. In the early days of Sandy's it would have been untruthful to endorse this claim for coffee. For then it was far from good. For months, Kenelm Foss racked his brains and those of other people to seek a solution of the difficulty. The major problem was how to keep

the milk hot yet prevent the formation of that thick
scum which is the product of milk that is boiled and
reboiled and reboiled. The milk had to be kept hot
because people would flock into Sandy's and demand
coffee immediately. Perhaps groups of twenty or
thirty people at a time. After all, Sandy's is not a
huge teashop where coffee is being drunk in vast
quantities all day long. At last Mr. Foss found the
solution. New urns of an improved type were
installed, and Sandy's proud boast as to the excellence
of the coffee served is now justified to the hilt.

The price of coffee is fourpence. It is not served in
" cups " ; but in thick, rather ugly white mugs,
invariably chipped : but who minds a little thing like
a chip or two ? It is astounding that there are any
mugs left at the end of a day : when you see the
rough usage they get from some careless customers.

The prices here, for sandwiches, were such that the
place would be bankrupt were it in New York.
Americans are quite willing to pay highly and " through
the nose," but they like to get what they consider to
be value for money.

Some years ago I described a typical Sandy's sandwich to a New York stenographer and asked her what
would be the right price to pay for it.

" A dime," she said. " If anyone was sucker
enough to pay that for such a sandwich in the type
of joint you've described."

A dime. Ten cents. Fivepence at par. Sandy's used to charge one shilling. But Mr. Kenelm Foss being an astute business man, and having a kind heart, took heed of the Depression—and down came the prices.

It is rather extraordinary that so many out-of-work chorus girls go to Sandy's. Professional dancing partners from night clubs, and other semi-pretty gamines of this 'ard, cruel world. How is it, that they can afford to pay the prices asked? It cannot be that they go to Sandy's thinking that young college lads will drift in and pay for their " coffee and " then take them out for a drive in a car. Oh no! Surely that could not be the reason?

Again, it is not possible that these girls should think they are the lure for a certain type of middle-aged man, who is almost certain to come along and "fix up the bill." Quite unthinkable.

Whatever you order at Sandy's comes to you in sandwich form. You could go through a six-course dinner—entirely in sandwiches. At the end of which you'd feel so much like a loaf, that you would automatically spread butter on yourself. If you did anything so foolhardy as try this six-course dinner idea, I have one bit of advice to offer you. Make a speedy pilgrimage to Boots' in Piccadilly Circus, just around the corner, and have them give you one emetic and one—something else; and I don't mean " sedative " either.

It is unnecessary for me to give you the names of

35　　　　　　　　　　　D

any of the varieties of sandwiches. There's always a bewildering selection ready on the counter ; there are many Daily Specials : there's an imposing list of sandwiches " made to order " : and, should you feel in mood to be yet more pernickety, you can get hold of the full list of one hundred and twenty varieties and make your choice from that. Probably you will be too overwhelmed by such an imposing array, and do as many other sensible folk do—leave it to the barman to choose a sandwich to accord with your mood of the moment.

In spite of the fussings and fumings of the Sandwich Bar dissenters, there is, without doubt, a real niche in the scheme of life for such places. For there are occasions when one finds that a sandwich and " cupper corfee " just hits the mark. But such comestibles have to be good : they have to be priced rightly : they have to be engulfed in surroundings that are clean and pleasant—not to say congenial.

Sandy's fulfils those requirements absolutely.

EATS LTD., 14, *Gerrard Street*, W.1.

There are times aplenty when you may want to go to a place of the sandwich bar genus, and yet be able to order something more positive than a sandwich. There is Eats, in Gerrard Street ; which combines snacks and sandwiches with light meals. Therefore, rather a " superior " kind of place.

It functions from nine o'clock one morning until

one o'clock the next. It is decorated in a pleasantly modern way, without being garish or startling: the food you get is good: the prices are most reasonable; and the service, except at the rush hours, perfectly satisfactory.

Incidentally, and other snack bars please take note, Eats serves a three-course table d'hôte luncheon. Though there are many people who are not interested in table d'hôte meals at snack bars, yet the menu of such at this place is calculated to fill a long-felt want for those ladies and gentlemen of the stage who want a decent meal at two shillings.

Here is a specimen menu: worthy of recording because it is oh-so-English:

Potato Soup.

———

Grilled Lamb Cutlet and Tomato.
Roast Beef and Yorkshire Pudding.
Braised Ham and Spinach.

Cold.
Ham and Tongue and Salad.
Roast Beef and Potato Salad.

———

Mashed Potatoes.
Baked Potatoes.
Spring Greens.
Spinach.

———

Baked Jam Roll.
Pineapple and Cream.
Waffle and Maple Syrup.

On the à la carte menu, there is a grand total of three hundred and thirty-two items (332). My familiarity with this and the glibness with which I produce the number " out of a hat " is due to the fact that every item on the menu is numbered. A very sensible idea, being helpful to customer and waitress alike. And the list itself is subdivided into Sandwiches, Cold Snacks, Appetizers, Soup, Grill, Salads, Vegetables, Omelettes, Savouries, Egg Dishes, Cheese, Sweets, Beverages, Minerals, and Sundries.

Item No. 203 reads, " Dates : stoned and cream." Rather funny.

Yet, on all this menu, I can find no mention of either Coca Cola or Waffles : two specialities in which Eats excels. There's no drink in the world so cooling as an iced Coca Cola with, perhaps, a dash or soupçon of gin. Americans in search of their beloved " Coke " will find it at Eats only, in London.

The young man at the back of this enterprise is one Ralph Munday. One-time pilot in the Royal Air Force, he also did stunt flying at Hendon on the occasions of the Royal Air Force Pageants. Now he buys eggs and bread and groceries wholesale : engages and dismisses waitresses : arranges table d'hôte luncheons. Not only does he do these things but he likes doing them : and does them well. Well, it's a queer world.

HONEYDEW, *Strand*, W.C.2.

This place takes its name from a drink of that name. The recipe of the drink is a secret : though its main ingredient is orange juice. Its joys are that it is cool and refreshing.

Honeydew—the place—is as white-tiled and spick and span as a newly-opened public swimming baths.

Canadian in origin, it introduced to Londoners all the thrills of super-cleanliness, super-hygiene and super-Self-Service.

Honeydew—the drink—is the main attraction. The entire menu of the place is as follows :

Honeydew (also in containers to take out).

Sandwiches of egg, salmon, cheese or ham in white or brown bread, toasted or plain.

Tea.

Coffee with cream.

Apple or raisin pie—Canadian style.

On Mondays and Tuesdays there's a speciality sandwich of minced ham and sweet pickle.

Wednesdays, Thursdays and Fridays, you can get home-made meat-and-potato pies. " Say, buddy ! They're swell ! Just like mother used to make ! "

There you are, then. Help yourself. You have to, anyway—at Honeydew.

39

LE GRILL CAUCASIEN, *Hotel Splendide, Piccadilly, W.1.*

Along Piccadilly where that thoroughfare acts as boundary to the Green Park, there is an imposing array of clubs. There are one or two automobile show-rooms : some small shops, and two hotels. One of these latter—the smaller, less conspicuous, more ex-clusive—is the Hotel Splendide. Hotel Splendide !

Its name savours of those cheap and dingy pensions in the back streets of Geneva and Monte Carlo. How much nicer to have left the Splendide with its former name of Green Park Hotel : so appropriate also, as this hotel looks over the park of that name. But Hotel Splendide !

The decorations of the suites are sumptuous. (For years I've wanted to use the word, but never until now has the description of anything justified it !)

Le Grill Caucasien, to most people, is the high spot of this hotel : simply because it happens to be well known and well patronized. It's under the personal management of Captain V. Vivien who ran the Kas-bek : and what he does not know about entertainment à la russe could be written on the edge of a postage stamp.

Always have I liked the soft lounge seats of this Grill : nearly as much as I mislike me of the soft lounge lizards sometimes seen basking on them in the glow of a wealthy patronne's pocket-book.

Captain Vivien is an artful man. He has contrived an atmosphere that one would swear to be Russian— provided that one had never been to the Land of the Bear. Stained-glass windows : oh-so-discreet lighting : thick carpets : waiters, to whom you can speak in Turkish and be answered correctly in Hungarian or any other language dictated by your fancy or the bottle.

So much for a general idea of the place.

Then there is a Cossack orchestra and choir. You know the sort of thing perfectly well ; either groaning from the bottom of their Russian boots, or making weird whoopee noises through the tops of their Russian hats. Cossack orchestra and choir—synonymous with " no middle course." I have a theory that all those weirdly-shaped balalaika instruments are bluff ; that they are all tuned and played exactly in the same way as mandolins and 'cellos. The strange shapes are intended to bemuse Western minds. Maybe not.

Then the food ! Thank goodness, the Grill Caucasien is not so exclusive that one may not eat. For there is nothing so intriguing to the palate as Russian food when properly prepared and served—as it is here. The food. Just read the following, which was Captain Vivien's description of a dish, as we sat together at luncheon :

" Schashlich d'agneau ? Schashlich ? Why, when I goh to a rest'rant and ask for them, they bring me, what ? Ugh ! 'Orrible things all 'ard and dried. Now here ! Ah ! We have it as it should be ! Look !

We jost take the lean pieces of saddle of lamb ; put them on a long, wooden skewer, see ? A piece of lamb kidney at each end : so ! Then greel them over a red coal-fire—so ! Give them a twist this way—and anodder twist that way : so ! Keep them moving. On the hop ! The pieces of lamb should be well done outside so as to keep the juice from ronning ouht : but inside it should be peenk. Jost peenk.—Try them ! "

I did. As he said, they were well done on the out-side ; and inside, all juicy and peenk : " jost peenk." This perfection in the art of grilling lamb is doubtless the product of evolution. For it is difficult to imagine hairy sons of the Steppes twisting a skewer this way : then " anodder twist that way : so " and keeping in mind all the time that the inside of the meat must be peenk.

Do you remember, O Mischa, of Sadko Restaurant in New York, those blinis we had ? They do them differently here—and to my way of thinking much, much better too.

Now the usual way of serving blinis is, first put a piping hot pancake on the plate ; then a great dollop of butter ; caviar, as ad lib as the management will tolerate ; more butter ; a final pancake. Apparently that is quite the wrong way of doing it. Just as wrong as it would be to eat them with chopsticks.

For the caviar, to be correct, must be eaten as cold as it is possible to make it. Slopping it on the hot pancake. . . . " Ugh! No, no, no, no, no!" says Captain Vivien. "The way blinis should be eaten is like this. Very hot blinis on one plate : very cold caviar on anodder. Take a piece of blini and just as you are going to eat it, put on a bit of caviar : so!" And we did.

You can get vodka here. A fiery drink. A drink to which one has to be educated ; it being thought ten degrees less palatable than "red Biddy." But then, an apprenticeship of bootleg vodka in New York may account for my dislike of any vodka, anywhere. That, however, does not lessen my admiration for those Russians, Royalist and Bolshevik, who pour this liquid fire down their asbestos throats.

Nor must it be overlooked, by the way, that the Grill Caucasien is a good place to dance. For, in addition to Cossack what nots, there is a dance band. Nothing special about it : just a dance band, but it marks good rhythm and does not offend.

Another brandy with you, Captain Vivien? Well, since you insist.

PICCADILLY HOTEL, *Piccadilly, W.1.*

Perhaps this is one of the best-known places of entertainment anywhere. Not that it tries to "set the world on its ear" with startling and freakish exhibitions or the like. Far from it. The Piccadilly is a quiet, dignified place, having a charm bred of mellowness. "Mellowness" does not, in any way, imply fustiness.

43

Far from it. Everything at the Piccadilly is of the most modern and absolutely up to date.

Let's deal with the frivolity side first. There is the Louis XIV Restaurant and the Grill Room. You can get table d'hôte luncheon for five-and-six : theatre dinner for seven-and-six : " dancing dinner " for ten-and-six, and " dancing supper " for the same price—needless to say, you get them in French.

There are " dancing teas " on Saturday and Sunday for five shillings. Which, being a rather high price, ensures a nice crowd of people.

The Grill Room prices are slightly lower. Luncheon, four-and-six : theatre dinner, five-and-six : " dancing dinner," seven-and-six.

In the restaurant there are two cabaret shows nightly : at dinner and supper. In the Grill Room the show is scheduled for 11.30 p.m. You can do your own floor show in either place as from nine o'clock.

What is really a joy is, that in the Grill Room evening dress or any other form of passable attire is correct. Whilst one may be a believer in the creaking shirt and choking collar for evening wear, it is nice to know that one doesn't have to don the beastly things. So the Grill Room is a haven to those weary people who want eye-and-ear entertainment without fuss.

There are two dance bands. Sydney Kyte in the restaurant and Jerry Hoey in the Grill Room. There is also a couple of orchestras sculling around the hotel at various times of the day, but they are of no concern to us at this juncture. Wagner and caviar sandwiches do not appeal as a blend.

Vairo, the Grill Room manager, is one of the suavest of people in the world. It's impossible to put him off his balance. I know. For one evening, after being fussy as to which table I would have, I demanded one poached egg for dinner : and got it. Vairo never turned a hair : and the service was as perfect as though I had ordered an elaborate and expensive dinner.

Oh, by the way, here's a little item which is an indication of the Piccadilly's perfection in service. If anyone approaching a table might be an American, the first thing done is to put a large jug of ice-water before him. It's those little courtesies which have made this delightful hotel remembered with affection by our confrères over the herring-pond.

Now let us give our considered attention to the delights of the table. Poached eggs on toast is not my unvarying choice of a dinner in the Grill Room. Why should it be ? The menu has selections from at least seven different countries famed for cuisine. It is representative of those cuisines at their best, too.

Visiting Americans are delighted to find such items as " Sweet Corn on the Cob ; " " Minced beef, Baltimore style ; " " Chicken à la King ; " and—stand to attention, O ye from the Land of the Free—" Corned Beef Hash ! "

I have personal memories of sweetbread cooked with a delightful cream sauce : such as can be found nowhere else in London.

Then, here are two recipes for which I can vouch. Lieut.-Col. Elwy-Jones, who is Social Manager of the Piccadilly, made me sit down and try them. How glad I am that he was so firm-minded !

Veal Cutlet " Bitter Sweet."

Fry a veal cutlet in butter. When fully cooked put aside. Take butter in which it was cooked, add a little more butter and bring to a foam. Add a tea-spoonful of vinegar, a dessertspoonful of castor sugar and some capers.

When this is thoroughly hot, stir well and allow the cutlet to simmer in it for a few moments. Serve very hot.

Poire Frédérique.

Peel and core a ripe pear. Remove from the bottom the interior of the pear and fill the cavity with a paste of marrons glacé. Make a sauce of Bar le Duc confiture (which can be bought in bottles) and Kirsch. Pour over pear and serve cold.

I should like to know in what way Noel Coward was responsible for the naming of the first recipe. Or if it was called " Bitter Sweet " just by way of being a compliment to him.

If you like pears, marrons glacé and Bar le Duc, all

of which most people do, there is no dessert in the world to equal the Poire Frédérique. Even if you are not sure, you soon will be, after eating it.

It is difficult for me to write glibly of the Piccadilly. So many memories are connected with it. Do take my advice, however : it is a good place to go. You'll like the friendliness of the atmosphere in conjunction with the excellence of everything the place offers.

Just look at this menu for a " dancing dinner."

DINER DANSANT.

7s. 6d.

Hors-d'Œuvre Variés.
Grape Fruit.

Consommé Yvette.   Consommé en Tasse.
Crème Voisin.   Crème de Tomates.

Suprême de Turbotin St. Valéry.
Délice de Sole Véronique.
Blanchailles Diablées au Poivre Noir.

Jambon Braisé au Xérès.
Vol-au-Vent Royale.   Tournedos Sauté Favorite.
Poussin en Casserole Chez-Soi.
Salade de Saison.

Coupe Dame Blanche.   Abricots Bourdaloue.
Compôte de Fruits.
Mignardises.

Most particularly would I wish to call your notice

to the hors-d'œuvre. These do not consist of a tired sardine, flatulent Bismarck herring, gangrenous-looking mussels, allied to an assortment of unappetizing salads. Instead, they are piquant little dishes set out to be a joy to the eye first of all, and then a stimulating comfort to the stomach. Don't miss them.

On your way out perhaps just a final drink in the American bar before letting yourself loose in the traffic of Piccadilly. . . .

TED SHACKLADY'S. (*West of Suez—just!*)

Many years ago work entailed my daily presence in the East End of London : yes ; east of Aldgate Pump and a great deal farther than Gardiner's Corner.

A low murky kind of work, necessitating my wearing garments which could not be described as elegant. I flatter myself that I looked just as tough as my fellow coal-shovellers. We were engaged in shovelling coal : hence we were coal-shovellers. " Low " work, because it meant back-breaking stooping : " murky " work, because coal is murky.

What a way to develop a truly gargantuan appetite. Too bad that such could not be assuaged with wondrous viands. The East End does not cater to coal-shovellers of æsthetic tastes.

So I had to snoop around for some place to eat. I found it.

Quite close to the docks is the Blackwall Tunnel :

quite close to the northern end of this man-made rabbit hole, is an eating-place called Ted Shacklady's. By the door is a blackboard on which is chalked such legends as " Pork and veg.," " Beef and pot.," " Tea : 1*d*." The upper half of the window space is allocated to the display of posters for local cinemas and other flea-palaces. The lower half of the window has a selection of foods in various stages of cooking. Even as you watch, a sausage bursts slowly (I mean that) and displays its innards to your fascinated gaze. Well-pressed cabbage—even as at the more refeened Simpson's—squats sulkily in an adjacent pan. Tomatoes, defiantly scarlet, frizzle, sizzle and hizzle next to that.

Inside ? Ah ! Now this is where you have to be strong-minded.

There are some four rough, rickety, plain deal tables —benches to sit on—nightmare containers for salt and pepper—vinegar bottles encrusted with the dirt of years—mustard in old broken cups—and an atmosphere that defies all description. It's . . . it's . . . well, if you insist on knowing what it's like, you must find out for yourself.

To the lady by the counter you give your order. And make it brief, and bereft of polysyllables : deliver it in that curiously clipped half-jocular, quarter-leering, quarter-respectful manner of address common to the rougher male element when addressing a " lidy."

When it's cooked, the food—meat, vegetable, gravy

and bread—is all shovelled (ominous word) on to one plate and that bloomped on to the table in front of you.

The fare is simple : none more so. It's English : yes. But it is cooked rightly and it is piping hot, and you do get one heck of a lot for your money. Tea and coffee—that's what Ted Shacklady names his hot beverages—are served in huge thick mugs.

I've eaten and drunk myself to a standstill for 1s. 2d. ; and that after eight hours of . . . exactly, I'll not mention it again.

If you do happen to be in that part of London : if you are suitably attired : if you're raging with hunger : if you have very little money—then go to Ted Shacklady's. Otherwise, keep away. This restaurant is not for the usual run of nice people who buy this book— by which I mean you ; and you ; and you.

ISOLA BELLA, 15, *Frith Street, W.1.*

At Isola Bella Restaurant you have one of those quieter, less obtrusive Italian restaurants. Would that there were more like this place flourishing under the ægis of the two Micottis.

Signor Micotti—is it E. Micotti or P. Micotti ?—is proud of the fact that the cooking of his restaurant has won medals and palms at Bruxelles, Nice, Firenze and Padova (those last two being Florence and Padua—to those who have not studied Continental time-tables).

He is proud, too, of the modernistic wall decorations : pictures in oil, and definitely crude to my un-tutored eye, are hung in recessed panels. Soft light-ing, thank goodness, prevails at Isola Bella.

It used to be a favourite haunt of mine—at least three times a week I could be found seated always at the same window table upstairs. At least once a week I had precisely the same meal. Escaloppe of veal with a half-portion of *Tagliatelli alla Bolognese* ; followed by a vanilla soufflé. For soufflés of all kinds this restaurant deserves to be more widely known than it is. No-where else have I discovered such light, evanescent con-coctions, be they chocolate, lemon, vanilla or of any other flavour.

On other occasions I browsed through the menu ; betraying a truly amazing catholicity of choice. Egg dishes, fish, entrées, grills : no matter what I tried it was always excellent. It is not easy for a small res-taurant of Isola Bella's calibre to be so undeviatingly good in all departments. After all, Signor Micotti has won medals and what not, so perhaps the reliability is not so amazing.

Once I found a soft and mushy radish or two : the horrified expression on the waiter's face was consola-tion enough, however.

Isola Bella has inaugurated a table d'hôte luncheon recently. A practice which seems to be becoming prev-alent with the greater number of London's restaurants. Still, as the choice is so varied, and the items are of such diversity, it is elementary justice to give a specimen menu. If in doubt, or feeling peevish and disinclined to think much about your food, you won't go far wrong in choosing from the table d'hôte.

The price of this three-course meal is three shillings and sixpence, including cover charge. Whilst this may not be the cheapest luncheon in Soho, undoubtedly 'tis one of the best values.

You are sceptical?

All right: read this menu, and you will become a believer.

TROIS COURSES AU CHOIX

Les hors-d'œuvre assortis.
Les omelettes aux fines herbes.
Les blanchailles diablées.
Minestrone à l'Italienne.
Les tagliatelle bolognese.

———

Le doube de bœuf provençale.
Les crepinettes de poulet Milanaise.
Le jambon grillé au petit pois.
Le chump chop à la sassi.
Le vol-au-vent à la reine.
Le fritto misto de la maison.

———

La coupe Alexandre.
Les crèpes au citron.
Les beignets de pommes.
Le roche de glace Hélène.
Le pot de crème vanille.
Les Welsh rarebit.
Les fromages assortis.

Well, that's all right as far as luncheon is concerned. Now, supposing you let me choose for you a dinner for two, to be in keeping with the Italian atmosphere, and yet having rather more " chic " than can be associated with spaghetti.

First of all, here are the items and the prices.

	s.	d.
Lobster cocktail (2 at 3s.) .	6	0
Entrecote à la Planche (for two)	7	0
Zambaglione al Marsala (2 at 1s. 6d.)	3	0
Mascarpone (2 at 1s. 3d.) .	2	6
	18	6

With this, a flask of Isola Bella's " Special Reserve " Chianti, if you can persuade Signor Micotti to part with one !

Now for a description of the items in the little dinner I have outlined above.

Lobster cocktail.

The lobster is cut into slices, sprinkled over with a mixture of hard-boiled eggs and aromatic herbs and served with a light pink cocktail sauce in champagne glasses.

Entrecote à la planche.

This is a sirloin thick steak, cooked and served on a special wooden plank, and surrounded with several kinds of primeur vegetables with a delicious red wine and mushroom sauce.

Zambaglione al marsala.

A froth-like hot custard served in silver cups, scented with Marsala wine and served with some special Italian macaroons (Amaretti). It is a light sweet and a very good stimulant.

These descriptions are Signor Micotti's own; and I'm intrigued by the last four words : " a very good stimulant." What does he mean?

Regarding mascarpone. This is a speciality so exclusive to Isola Bella that I had to be shown how one eats it : now that I have developed a first-class mascarpone-technique, let me teach you.

Mascarpone is the name of the Isola Bella Special Cream Cheese. Only it's rather more than cream and yet not quite cheese. A portion arrives, wrapped in muslin : rather coy. Undressing the pallid mascarpone, the next step is to squash, mash and otherwise spread it about the plate, with a fork. A little castor sugar is then sprinkled on it. Now comes the fun! After the sugar, sprinkle one of four flavours in powdered form : chocolate, cinnamon, coffee or ginger. (Chocolate is best.) Not too much : just a small teaspoonful. Beat the powder and sugar into the mascarpone ; eat ; give thanks unto whatever gods you worship that you have learnt a new dish that is so good.

The mascarpone comes from near Milan ; and as detailed above, is an odds-on favourite with the Milanese—well, the Milanese are nobody's fools. They know a thing or two.

Although this restaurant is not in the cheap class, when once you have eaten there you'll admit that the prices are fully justified.

By the way, may I suggest that you ask for my pet waiter there : Bettacini by name ? It was a delight to see him back again, after his seafaring exploits as a steward aboard some mammoth liner.

Denman Street, W.1.

This thoroughfare must be at least sixty yards in length. It's near Piccadilly Circus. In fact, is the first turning on the north side of Shaftesbury Avenue : it ends at the luggage entrance of the Regent Palace Hotel.

One claim to fame that Denman Street has, is that it includes the address of a huge garage ; also of a musical instrument shop and Band Rehearsal Studios —from which latter come the most amazing bursts of music to delight or offend the ears of lazy Londoners.

Another claim to fame is this. Should you elect to feed at an eating-place in this street : should you elect to become temperamental and refuse to pay your bill : should the proprietor elect to throw you out very forcibly " on your neck," what would happen ? The chances are fifty to one that you would hurtle through some doorway and alight at a table in another eating-place. Denman Street is so chock-a-block with them.

From Shaftesbury Avenue, walking up the left-hand side : first of all, the back entrance to Maison Lyons : then the Oriental Café ; Marie Elizabeth Waffle Bar ; public-house. Going up the other side, there is first of all a public-house ; then the Denman Snack Café ; the Troika ; Abrahamson's Kosher Restaurant ; S.F. Snack Bar ; Mrs. Cook's ; another public-house.

Just eleven of them : and all making a living.

After marvelling at this awhile, why not go through the swing doors of the Regent Palace Hotel and spend half an hour in the lobby ?

" Half an hour doing what ? " you ask.

Counting house detectives, of course. One of London's more popular amusements for rainy days.

RESTAURANT BOULESTIN, 25, *Southampton Street, Strand, W.C.2.*

There are in London a few—very few—restaurants where the art of French cooking has been raised to the *n*th degree of perfection. I know of three, myself : one is in Soho, another, not a hundred yards from Dover Street Station, and the third is the Restaurant Boulestin, presided over by the one and only M. Xavier Marcel Boulestin.

Had I any real discretion, I'd choose one of the other

two : for M. Boulestin is not only a prince of restaurateurs, a connoisseur *par excellence* of food, but a
writer of no mean merit. However, if I make any
mistakes ; if I do not always speak of my subject with
the reverence and solemnity it deserves, perhaps M.
Boulestin will forgive me—as being a mere blundering
Englishman who " means well " ?

M. Boulestin maintains that food should be eaten
amid surroundings of red plush and muslin curtains.
No flowers on the table. In such circumstances, there
can be nothing to distract the attention from the food.
Then the lighting should be really good, brilliant, in
fact ; so that a man can see what he eats.

Why not carry that idea a step farther ? Everyone
who comes to a restaurant should be put into a plain
wooden stall by himself or herself : illumination provided by a miniature searchlight.

Well, whatever the good proprietor chooses to say
concerning surroundings, he does not carry out his uncomfortable ideas at the Restaurant Boulestin. The
chief colour—it cannot be called " dominant "—is a
warm golden brown : pleasing and not distracting.
The curtains are not of muslin—nor of any other
material at " one-eleven-three " a yard.

There are no flowers on the tables.

This restaurant is definitely one of the most expensive in London. There are reasons for it. The prices
are not high in order to make the place " chic," but

because every detail of the food is so studied that only perfection may result.

One point is, that the butter used in the kitchen is exactly the same as that in the little stone pots on the table. The cream in the sauce is the best fresh cream procurable. Everything in the way of food is the pick of the market. Every dish, no matter what, is freshly prepared and cooked for each customer.

Those are some of the reasons why prices are high at this restaurant. It is a place where one lunches and dines : not eats. What a world of difference that is !

As M. Boulestin remarks quite nonchalantly, " You can get an excellent luncheon of hors-d'œuvre, the plat du jour and cheese for six or seven shillings." True enough : and after you've had it you realize that the price is not excessive. The hors-d'œuvre are models of perfection, with many varieties that I dare swear are unknown to you. The *plat du jour* is an item from a wide range of choice. The cheese, no matter which kind you choose, is always at its most delectable.

Maybe you think that the prices of the wines are so high that you have to read them with a telescope ? Then you are going to be pleasantly surprised. There is a delightful pink wine of Touraine at only five shillings and sixpence a bottle. There are other Loire wines from as low as four-and-six a bottle. Such prices are far from prohibitive.

For those who like champagne, yet deplore its superfizziness, there is Champagne Nature costing about twelve shillings a bottle. It has all the qualities and properties of the champagne more generally known, but it has not been doctored in any way. By all means try this Champagne Nature.

Among liqueurs. M. Boulestin has some of those extremely unusual ones such as Calvados, Quetsch and Mirabelle. Other restaurants there are that may keep one of these—according to which is the liqueur of the proprietor's home province. But here, you get them all. They are, in simple language, brandies distilled from different fruits, even as Cognac is from the grape. They preserve, magically, the essence and humour of the various fruits. And are they potent !

Clarets are served at the temperature of the room : Burgundies and Côtes du Rhône at cellar-temperature : all white wines slightly iced.

What about " vins rosés," M. Boulestin ?

This restaurant has conceded to fashion inasmuch as it serves a theatre dinner, table d'hôte. There is a considerable range of choice, and to help those diners who may be feeling more than usually incompetent, there is a specimen table d'hôte already chosen—and displayed at the top left-hand corner of the menu.

Don't try to get this theatre dinner at 8.30 p.m. You will be met with looks of blank astonishment. M. Boulestin knows perfectly what time the shows begin in London !

Now here is a specimen dinner chosen by M. Boulestin which, if ordered beforehand and for not fewer than four people, would cost fifteen shillings and sixpence a head. That is not so dear considering the style, quality and quantity.

> Potage Germiny.
> Filets de sole véron.
> Canard au chambertin.
> Pommes soufflées.
> Crêpes verlaine.

These last are pancakes, which are twiddled around in much the same way as Crêpes Suzette : only absinthe is the keynote.

Of one thing you can be well assured. That when you dine or lunch at this restaurant you will come away with a delightful glow : a mellow feeling that all is very well indeed with the world. For M. Boulestin is an artist in food : and believes in his art thoroughly.

Wind up a perfect dinner with a glass of Quetsch, is sound advice.

Try out these recipes on your own kitchen range.

Filets de sole véron.

Make a good Béarnaise sauce well flavoured with Tarragone, to which you add a tablespoonful of good tomato sauce. This sauce is to be served with fillets of sole sprinkled with breadcrumbs, which then should be cooked not only nicely brown in butter but literally swimming in butter. It gives the fish an incomparable richness which is happily counter-balanced by the pleasant sharpness and the spicy taste of the sauce.

Crèpes Nicole.

Have some legs and wings of chicken poached with carrots, onions and a bouquet of thyme, parsley and a bay leaf. When they are cooked cut them in small cubes, toss them lightly in butter, season and sprinkle well with paprika. Add a few fresh mushrooms pre-viously cooked, cut in pieces and mix with a little cream, just enough to moisten the mixture, and keep hot.

Prepare a good béchamel sauce and a few thin un-sweetened pancakes. Place on each pancake some of the mixture, roll it and arrange all the pancakes in a long fireproof dish. Add a yolk of egg to the béchamel sauce, a little cream, pour over the pan-cakes, sprinkle with grated cheese and brown under the grill. Serve at once.

This dish can be garnished with asparagus tops or slices of truffles according to season.

The preparation at home of such dishes will give any housewife plenty to think about! To make life still more pleasant for you, here's a " tip " from M. Marcel Boulestin, which I will pass on to you as being well worth while.

When lunching there, and you get to the cheese course, choose Brie. With it drink claret : Château Marquis-de-Terme, 1908 vintage. That's a recipe you'll be happy to try.

Speaking of other rabidly-French restaurants :

One is the *Basque* in Dover Street : considerably smaller than Boulestin so far as floor space is concerned : but not much smaller when it comes to the bill ; though the high prices are fully justified.

The other is *L'Escargot Bienvenu*, Greek Street, Soho. This place makes a speciality of French home-cooking. What the Germans describe so aptly as " Bürgerlich." Snails and frogs' legs are two of the specialities at this place. It is an excellent place to try, and its comfortable, home-like atmosphere is restful and soothing.

QUO VADIS RESTAURANT, 27, *Dean Street, W.*1.

Come other days when we may falter in the quest of restaurants that are uncompromisingly Italian or bigotedly French. Instead, by way of a holiday, let's seek for that hybrid product begotten of Italy and France and flourishing mightily in England.

There are several such that deserve careful mention ; and so far as it is possible I will do impartial justice by such as are included in this book for especial commendation.

Still in Soho. After gaping awhile at the posters

outside the Royalty Theatre in Dean Street and wondering if the " House Full " boards are true, we about-face ; and there in front of us is an inconspicuous though neat-of-appearance restaurant whose name asks plaintively, " Quo Vadis ? " Quo Vadis ? Surely there is but one answer and we make it. Dodging a Brooklands model sports car, and stepping over a swarm of children playing in the road, we pass through the doorway.

A certain air of restrained bustle is the first note struck by this place. Not unpleasing by any manner of means. Before your hat and coat are taken by Candida—for that is the lady's name—there is no doubt about it all ; this restaurant is actuated, though not dominated, by a personality. A restful welcoming one, at that.

Was it my intention to speak impartially of each restaurant ? Such is wellnigh impossible.

For, even after a first visit, one is liable to enthuse over Quo Vadis. It is one of those singularly rare places in London to which one can go again and again without getting fed up with it.

In writing of restaurants personal prejudice counts for a great deal. I have a " personal prejudice " in favour of the Quo Vadis restaurant. So has everyone else who goes thither.

The food, the service, the staff and the general atmosphere are all that they should be and so rarely are—

particularly is that combination of excellence a rarity in slovenly Soho.

What is it that engenders that feeling of well-being as one enters this restaurant ? The knowledge that perchance there may be something superlatively extraordinary in the way of cuisine ? Scarcely that ; for it would be difficult to find fault on that score, peevish carper though you may be. Because there may be rich and strange things to eat ? Not that exactly ; though there is a bewildering variety of things listed on the menu. These are not the causes of that " something different " at Leoni's. Ah ! Methinks that that's the answer. Leoni's. Rather than Quo Vadis one thinks of this restaurant by the name of its proprietor. Tribute of a kind, to the personality of friend Leoni.

Be introduced then, to our charming and courteous host, who cheers the place with the effulgence of his good nature. Who does a great deal more than that, i' faith. For he makes himself responsible for each and every dish that is prepared in the kitchen. Yes ; he supervises the cooking. Leoni has solved the problem of being in forty-four places at once ; it is one of the unrecorded miracles how he manages to be upstairs, downstairs, in the kitchen, and saying " au revoir " to people outside, all at one and the same time.

The personal interest he takes in the preparation of the dishes results in the good food that is put on the table for your enjoyment and for mine.

64

He won a Silver Medal for cooking in 1930. In so doing, lost his harassed look. Since then he has won the praise and admiration of countless people for precisely the same reason as brought him the medallion : excellent cuisine. No doubt about it ; there is a cuisine here worthy of your close and discriminating attention.

He has chosen his staff with the same care and deliberation that he gives to the choosing of his beefsteaks. Louis, *maître d'hôtel*, is, I suspect, of Basque origin. Which would account for his subtle and sardonic sense of humour. Ernest—who is English—and Tamborini, two waiters who attend my needs, have never yet been found wanting.

Would you like to meet also Raffaelo, Leoni's five-years son and heir, possessor of the longest eyelashes in London ? It is this young man who captures more feminine hearts than a Navarro or Chevalier.

This restaurant is the head-quarters of the Grubb Group of painters whose work is hung on the walls. You may like these pictures—and you may not. Whatever your taste in such matters, these mural decorations form a topic of conversation—if such be your need.

Enough ! Enough of this chatter ; let's eat !

For indeed there is food too good for mere kings in this restaurant ; it's for us, my friend ; for you and me.

Leoni introduced green tagliatelli to London : a

65

species of flat macaroni made verdant through the
agency of spinach. One meets this dish in Italy;
especially in such Florentine and Venetian restaurants
as cater for tourists. But 'twas Quo Vadis that
pioneered this decorative farinage in London. And
each order is made freshly; which is no light task,
but indicative of the great trouble to which Leoni will
go, to ensure the excellence of his cuisine.

Among other specialities of the place, can be named
these two: though only an experienced chef will be
able to produce the right dish, from these somewhat
indefinite instructions:

Truite à la Cleopatra.

(Was the Nile stocked with trout in Pharaoh
days?)

Trout cooked in butter, then covered with a sauce
made of " Courgette " (baby marrow) and Demi-
Glacé Tomatée.

(Does " marrow " mean vegetable marrow? I
hope so; for " baby " in conjunction with " marrow " smacks of charnel-house antics.)

Suprême de volaille à la Delysia.

The breast of Surrey chicken cooked in butter,
with fresh asparagus and English mushrooms spread
over the suprême, and the whole covered with a
delicious sauce composed of cream, butter, paprika
and a little of Bordeaux.

66

Now, if those recipes are too vague, the responsibility lies at Leoni's door. Go to Quo Vadis and ask for yourself what it's all about. One or two other specialities which really must be brought to your notice are *Lasagne Bolognesi* and *Filetti alla pappagallo*. Try them all, over and over again. They are indeed excellent.

Where would the Italian language be, without the word " alla " ? That Trout Cleopatra—ha ! There's a trout that Brillat Savarin would have appreciated.

As for wines. Well, Leoni has the usual run of Italian, French and German products. It is advisable, however, to be conservative enough to drink Chianti ; and at that, Chianti Medici, vintage 1923. The number on the wine list being " 7," if I recollect aright. It, too—the Chianti, not the number—has a personality.

There's no doubt about it. Here is a good place : one of the smaller restaurants offering excellent food and service at prices that are really reasonable.

Then, there are other Franco-Italian places, of course. Some yet more elegant than Quo Vadis ; others, that range downwards to the forthright dingy. Let's amble around and do a bit of exploring.

In a few words I'll dispose of quite a bunch.

AU PETIT SAVOYARD, 35, *Greek Street.*

Especially to be recommended is the delicious lobster salad : which with hock cup at 9.30 is the only way to pass a hot summer's evening. But you may have to wait a long time for that last-named essential of climate.

PETIT RICHE, 44, *Old Compton Street*,

has, perhaps, one of the most faithful and unchanging of clientèles in London. That is due to " Charlotte," who is the presiding genius of the place. In referring to her thus familiarly there is meant nothing of disrespect : she is known to all her well-satisfied customers as " Charlotte." How do these customers become well-satisfied ? On *Tournedos Petit Riche* without doubt. It is a good and attractively-arranged steak. Eat it.

THE CHANTECLER, 56, *Frith Street*.

This place really caters excellently well at low rates, specializing in table d'hôte luncheons and dinners.

Now, it is my personal idiosyncrasy to avoid those table d'hôte and à la carte restaurants that have set luncheons and dinners at a choice of prices. It may be because, many years ago, my father told me that these table d'hôte meals are composed of the leavings of other Soho restaurants. A little fiction which left its mark.

THE RENDEZVOUS, 45, *Dean Street*,

is just one of those places. And it was with considerable trepidation that I allowed myself to be guided thither.

Unreservedly, I admit my misgivings were unfounded. A look around the kitchens of this restaurant before luncheon, actually gave me an appetite. Not many Soho cooking-cubbies would bear such inspection and not fill me with disgust.

Here you get a really good luncheon for three shillings and dine on the same high plane for four. If you want to try something à la carte, try the Sole Rendezvous ; it is a dish to remember blissfully in your prayers.

There are other restaurants that belong to this same category. Too numerous to mention here : besides, it is pleasant to make discoveries for oneself —where restaurants are concerned. Soho is a happy hunting ground for the intrepid explorer and pioneer.

BELLOMETTI'S, 27, *Soho Square*, *W.1.*

Eighteen years past a waiter called Peppino, in a certain restaurant endeared himself to me by secreting apples and tangerines in my pockets. Then I lost touch of him, until that day not so long ago when I saw him at Bellometti's, which is at the Soho Square corner of Greek Street. Dear Peppino ! Now head waiter with squarely-tailored shoulders and the most amiable head waiter-y of smiles. Just the same ; not changed one jot in appearance.

So of course it was the order of the day to have

a grand luncheon to celebrate. To begin with, it would be as well to mention that this restaurant is one of the most chic of the Franco-Italian group. Therefore not so "ver cheep." However, the cooking and everything justifies the additional cost.

First of all, a very pale dry sherry. Surely, the pennies extra are a good expenditure for seeing the sherry poured from a little barrel that is wheeled to your table? This little ritual adds zest to the drinking of the sherry.

A lobster cocktail. Yes; the thought of such brings a shudder to those old Diehards who eat a "lobster on the hoof" as it were. But the cocktail sauce does not spoil the flavour of the lobster; brings it out rather.

Sole Bellometti. An intriguing conceit. Fillets of sole curled around a purée of lobster : over this, a mushroom sauce. The whole thing decorated by one prawn—only one—perched rakishly just where the sole's rump would be.

Tiny slivers of veal, sauté-d in Chablis, and with it, a few spikes, sticks, stalks or what-you-will of asparagus. This, and the sole before it, were cooked in fireproof dishes. A little trick which helps to make the food even more appetizing to the eye.

As a dessert, cold stewed pears with chocolate sauce —but no vanilla ice-cream.

Now that is rather a large luncheon; but then it

is not every day that one has a reunion with the rare Peppinos of this world.

To drink? Nothing but ice-water after the sherry. How American! No; how sensible, in view of the varied menu of the luncheon.

Bellometti's is distinctly a place to mark on your list with a big arrow.

Perhaps these three recipes may be of assistance to you in choosing a dinner. Two of them are of the items above: the third was really more than I could tackle in the same luncheon menu.

Filet de sole Enrico.

Filet de sole which has been opened and stuffed with lobster farce, folded up and poché, garnished with têtes de champignons, crevettes roses, truffles, and covered with a rich lobster sauce and glazed.

Escaloppé de veau maison.

Two fillets of veal, salt and pepper, and fry in butter and add French mushrooms, cut in small squares and cover with white wine and cream sauce.

Ris de veau Marcel.

Sweetbread braised and glazed, and garnished with fresh fond d'artichauts and financière in small squares.

Dear me! It seems I have made a crass mistake in saying that the fillets of sole curled around the lobster.

It's nothing of the kind. The lobster is pushed, willy-nilly, into the sole.

How much nicer " Crevettes roses " is than "pink prawns."

That Ris de Veau Marcel. You will have to take their word for it, that it's good ; myself I don't know, and after the luncheon I had there felt so plethoric that I don't want to know.

Let Peppino choose your wines for you ; he understands such things.

COFFEE-STALL CAPERS.

A feature of London's night life is the coffee-stall ; nicknamed " Hotel de Move Along " by waggish taxi-drivers.

No matter how many night clubs may open and be closed ; irrespective of whether there is a labouring Conservative party, or a conservative Labour party dominant in the Government ; uncaring as to Five-Year Plans in Russia ; the coffee-stalls of London are as much a part of that city's nightscape as the mad scamperings of lovelorn alley cats.

When night has come, the coffee-stalls, all primed and charged with comestibles, roll out of their slumber quarters, and are motor-towed, horse-drawn, pushed or pulled by hand to their respective " pitches."

Twiddle with the gardenia in the lapel of your coat : applaud the clever turns of a smart cabaret : the coffee-stall cares not—for it gets you as a customer later on.

When D.O.R.A. claps the lid on London's fun, just as you are beginning to feel really peppy, there are three things to do : go to bed, go to a dingy night-club, go to a coffee-stall.

Going to bed may be all very well. . . .

Who wants to be bored in a stupid, cheaply-vicious, tawdry night-club ? " Sucker joints " they call them in New York.

So let's go to a coffee-stall.

There are hundreds of them in London. Maybe I know a dozen or so. Out of that dozen, two know me. Out of those two, I like one. So come with me to the Gloucester Road Underground Station : right outside we'll find a coffee-stall run by a pair of brothers-in-law : Eddie and Louis. Those may not be their right names. Apropos of nothing at all, these youngsters have eight children between them. Maybe that proves that coffee-stall keeping is a healthy life.

The habitués of a coffee-stall can be divided into four groups. Taxi-drivers ; those who come " for a lark ; " those lonely ones who seek the comfort of human society in the wee sma' hours ; the serious-minded people who pursue their various avocations after dusk.

Of all the coffee-stalls I have visited, this one is the brightest, cleanest, most cheery one. The menu is more or less as follows :

Sandwiches of : saveloy (hot) ; ham ; egg ; cheese ; egg and tomato : at fourpence or sixpence.

Rock cakes ; doughnuts ; hot apple pies ; short-cake ; scones—some other kinds of cakes : twopence.

Chocolate.

Cigarettes.

Coffee, twopence a cup.

Tea, same price as coffee.

Bovril, fourpence.

And a special brew of particularly strong tea known as " literary tea : " a brew inaugurated by . . . I blush modestly.

Taxi-drivers are the mainstay of the place. Cheerful, chummy, jocular, they make fun of bad times and bad weather. What they don't know about horses and the ones that are going to win would fill a library. There are more " flopped " tips about horses given at coffee-stalls than in the rest of London.

There are the philosopher-taxi-drivers ; the well-read ones ; the " sporty " ones ; the lugubrious ones ; and . . . the ordinary, grumpy ones—though this latter is a rara avis at this stall. There's too friendly an atmosphere for grumpiness to last long.

Frankly, those young folk who go to coffee-stalls " for a lark " are a bit of a bore to the serious-minded people. " A lark," in their case, seems to consist of taking up all available space by the counter ; ordering the minimum ; and making the maximum noise—

together with fatuous inanities anent coffee-stalls ; wisecracks about draughts, and other remarks of similar pungency.

The third group can be distinguished easily. They are represented by silent young men and boys who hang about on the fringe of the coffee-stall crowd : they take a long time in consuming their orders and hope wistfully, though fearfully, that some one will speak to them—if only to pass the time of day.

Those who work by night include those darlings of the area steps—policemen. Nice, large, comforting chunks of humanity : who lose ninety per cent. of their awe-inspiring dignity if they remove their helmets for even a half-second. An occasional sleepy newspaper man. Railwaymen and bus-drivers. Sometimes the gentle sex is represented by those ladies of hard bargaining and—must I say it ?—easy virtue. Poor dears ! There's not much chance of picking up business at a coffee-stall. Then there are a few writers, who suffer from the delusion that they work best at night. (Time when this was written : 2.10 a.m.)

A motley crowd. Always changing its component parts, yet remaining much the same as a whole throughout the night : night after night for year after year.

Eddie and Louis—Louis is the one with the round face and only three children !—know me well. Or they should do by now. For whether I go a-wandering

75

in Canada, the United States of America, Central or Southern Europe or the Balkans, there is a ritual to be observed on my return to London.

" Good evening, Eddie ! Tea, please ! "

" Hullo ! Good evening ! Literary tea ? "

" Yes. How's things ? "

" Oh, much the same. Mustn't grumble."

Then just a little conversation as to what may be changed during an absence of a year—two years, or more.

'Tis a good place, this coffee-stall.

* * * * *

STOP PRESS NEWS. Since writing the above, Eddie or Louis—I don't know which—has become the father of another child. Two more, and they'll have their own Soccer team. It's a great life.

HOTELS

If it were really permissible to make use of expressive American slang, this section of the book would be entitled " Swell Dumps." But it does occur to me that maybe the Ritz, Claridge's and the Carlton would prefer not to be referred to as " dumps " no matter how " swell."

As it is, only a few of the major hotels can be treated with in this book. London is full of good hotels : no matter what a few disgruntled foreigners may say to the contrary. Those that have been selected are the ones most likely to appeal to the seeker of food, drink and entertainment. There is no personal reason of mine for those chosen : no axe to grind.

So it must be laid to the credit side of my balance sheet, that in order to get the material and the various excellent recipes that follow, I spent good hard-earned money ; just through being so conscientious—and you know how much authors make per annum . . . well, then.

First of all, the Ritz. That hostelry that says " Thus far, and no farther ! " to the Green Park. It would be wellnigh redundant to say much of this hotel—as an hotel : it is too well known to need superfluous comment. Though in the cause of exactitude it would be interesting to know if it's true of the American who was on a European " voyage aux vins," who, on recovering from his delirium tremens, looked at the pink and grey decorations of his bedroom and said, " Ah ! the Ritz ! Now am I in London, Paris, or Madrid ? " I hope it's a libel so far as Madrid is concerned—never having been there.

It is a fact none the less, that the Ritz Hotels in this world have achieved and maintain a monotonously high standard of, well, " Ritziness ! " They have become a measuring-glass of excellence ; even as Rolls-Royce is for automobiles.

Of the Ritz in London, however. Although the

grill room is underground, it gets plenty of fresh air from the park. Which is a blessing. You don't have to shout; because the band has to play its sad music in a far-away corner. Maybe that's why it sounds sad; it feels it has been ostracized. So whispering gently to the waiter, order Filet de Sole Aida, which has an iced white wine sauce and other things to tickle your palate. Perhaps you can persuade the band to play the appropriate music.

The sole should be followed—at a proper and respectful interval—by Poularde Chevalière. Just a feminine Maurice, eh? Still, it is delicious; but then this particular combination of mushrooms and truffles could not fail to arouse your enthusiasm.

HOTEL METROPOLE.

Do you remember the old, old days of the Midnight Follies at the Metropole? You do? Well, let's go to the Hotel Metropole; for, though the Midnight Follies are no longer extant, Monsieur Charles Kuhn, the chef, is very much alive. He knows a thing or two about " cheffing."

First of all, two special recipes which appeal to the mind on account of the names. Cecilia sounds saintly for soles: "Capucine " as applied to chickens seems right to me—the monks have always had a reputation for being good cooks.

Try doing these, when you are pressed for time!

Délice de Sole Cecilia.

Fillets of sole fried crisp in butter with a little olive oil. Dish up with prawns and little asparagus heads. Squeeze lemon-juice over fillets, and finish by adding a brown butter over them. Put a light cordon of anchovy sauce round the fillets. When serving, sprinkle chopped parsley and yolk of hard-boiled egg over all.

Fricassé de Volaille Capucine.

Take a young Surrey chicken and separate the wings, legs, breast, etc. Season with salt and pepper. Place in saucepan with small silver onions and button mushrooms. Cover with white wine, small glass of brandy and white stock, and bring to the boil. When the chicken is cooked, remove it, but keep it hot. Make sauce with remaining stock, adding a little flour, butter and fresh cream, with the yolk of an egg. Pour sauce through a fine strainer over chicken, and serve with pilau rice as garniture.

Now recipes written out as these two, have a straightaway appeal to the gastronome, so much so that it is difficult not to try your hand at making the dishes. It is to be hoped you will have a success with these confections : it is a matter of history that I did not. However, the very wise people will steer an undeviating course for the Hotel Metropole, when desirous of eating Fricassé de Volaille Capucine. It is pleasant to know that Mr. Kuhn is somewhere in the offing, to supervise the intricacies of such culinary masterpieces.

No ; the Metropole is far from cheap—but, ye gods ! it's good. They believe in table d'hôte dinners of nine courses. A mere trifle.

Just see what you get in the way of a mere trifle.

DINNER MENU

Caviar de Beluga aux Blinis.

———

Consommé Double au Nid d'Hirondelles.
Crème Reine-Margot.

———

Truite Saumonée Carmencita.

———

Mignonnette d'Agneau Pompadour.
Pommes Nana.
Petits Pois Frais à la Menthe.

———

Poussin en Cocotte Cyclamen.
Salade Favorite.

———

Asperges Lauris Sauce Mousse d'Or.

———

Soufflé Glacé Fleurette.
Corbeille de Mignardises.

———

Dessert.

———

Café.

If you are a bit peckish and feel you'd like a quick snack before going to an early show, the Metropole

caters to your needs in serving a Theatre Dinner.
Just a mouthful. Only seven courses. Seven courses
—why, it's hardly worth while sitting down to it.
No : stick to the proper dinner, my boy, and let the
flibbertigibbety weaklings have their theatre dinner.

Three courses, or four at the most, is the limit for
most people. But that is no reason why, every now
and then, you should not sit down and tackle this nine-
course affair. It is an experience of a long, elaborate,
but well-balanced dinner.

Emilio Colombo's Band distils soft music calculated
to muffle the gasps and groans of diners who feel like
over-stuffed furniture.

The wine list here, although pretty to look upon and
containing 282 drinks from which to make your
choice, is fairly much the same as any other wine list,
which seems to be a " fade-out " in comparison with
the cuisine. To compensate, however, the prices are
reasonable ; the brands are well-known and reputable.
The wines will be served correctly—if you speak first
to Emile, the *maître d'hôtel*. There is a Moselle of
which you should make a note. Its number on the
wine list is 611 and the price 12s. 6d. per bottle.

With a liqueur or so, a little dinner for two can be a
most expensive affair at the Metropole. But worth it
every time. Very well worth it.

HOTEL VICTORIA.

This is no distance at all from the Metropole. As it happens, I lunched at the Victoria on the day after dining at the Metropole. These two hotels are under the same directorship.

Feeling jaundiced, I placed myself in the care of Louis, *maître d'hôtel*, who evolved a simple two-courses-and-coffee luncheon for me : at least, Louis considered it to be a simple luncheon.

The two courses were so intriguing that I was able to " sit up and take notice " and ask for the recipes. These were written out rapidly, what time excellent strong and hot black coffee was brought to my table.

Here are the recipes of Louis's " simple luncheon " dishes, copied out word for word.

Julienne de Sole Beaulieu.

Cut fillet of sole into small pieces. Put 4 oz. of butter in saucepan. Put fillet of sole into pan with Julienne of lobster with sliced mushroom. Let cook slowly together. Add to it some Devonshire cream, salt and pepper and fish glaze. When cooked, add 2 yolks of eggs and well mix up with the sauce. Put all into china dish and glaze. When the fish is glazed, add slices of tomatoes just cooked in butter and tops of asparagus and one hard-boiled egg chopped on top of asparagus and tomatoes and leave for a few minutes in oven to get warm all together.

Noix de Ris de Veau Pecheresse.

Thread (clout) the sweetbread with truffle, tongue and lard. Put the sweetbread in saucepan with a little onion, carrots and roots of parsley and butter. Braise sweetbread and when nearly cooked add some sherry and glaze viande. Well baste with the stock to get the sweetbread a nice brown colour. When nearly cooked put into a cocotte. Add slice of foie gras and mushrooms and a quarter of a cooked artichoke. Put all stock from sweetbread on the whole dish, close it up firmly to avoid the air and leave in bain-marie in oven for ten minutes.

Sole and sweetbread. Both rich foods, yet so perfectly cooked and served that they acted as a tonic pick-me-up.

You will observe the use of the word " clout " in that second recipe.

Talking of soles. Are there any statistics available to show the annual London consumption of that genus ichthyoid ? If all the soles are genuine, then one should be able to walk across the Channel on the heads of Dover soles packed tightly together in a mad scramble to get on to Londoners' tables.

Actually, I believe half the soles that appear in draperies of sauce are really plaice and other flat fish.

What a touching picture.

Mother flat fish (*taking a shoal of offspring on to her knee*) : "And now, my dears, if you are very, very good indeed, you will grow up to be served as real soles ; and cost just the same price as our haughty relations near Dover !"

(*Intense jubilation on the part of flat fishlets who go to sleep without further bribes.*)

HOTEL MAYFAIR.

This is one of London's newer hotels, and needs no publicity boost from anyone, you may be sure. For it must be doing exceedingly well indeed. It is a very popular haunt of large numbers of the younger set. For the very good reason that Bert Ambrose and his band have developed a pretty technique calculated to make most people dance. There are people who profess, in all earnest, to be completely unstirred by Bert Ambrose's band. However, such strange folk are in the minority.

The food ! What a chef ! The man who invented these recipes that follow should be forbidden to leave London. Such genius must not be permitted to depart from our midst. You will observe that our old friend the sole figures in them ! In this case, I know they are genuine ; because I sat in the kitchen and watched the whole thing being done, and then scuttled back into the restaurant to eat them.

Suprême of Sole La Varenne.

Fillet of sole cooked in champagne and mushrooms, served with mousse of lobster in centre of dish, garnished with claws of the lobster. Cover fillets of sole with the sauce extracted from stock of the fillets of sole and of the mousse, and also with a creamed American sauce, extracted from the carapaces of lobster.

Volaille Veille Mode.

Cooked in paste, after being stuffed with mushrooms, truffles and lamb sweetbreads and mixed with a Sauce Allemande (white sauce); cut the suprêmes (breasts) in slices, rearrange on top and cover with cream sauce bound with foie gras.

These two courses, each perfection, are calculated to reduce one to a state of pop-eyed repletion.

Charles, *maître d'hôtel*, suggested I might like to try something " a little more substantial."

When he understood me to mean " no ! " he gave me the following recipe, which is reproduced herewith for your edification and suggested trial.

Gigot de Pauillas Maître Charles.

Braise a leg of spring lamb with Spanish onions, drain, when tepid cut in slices, reshape in layers with a paste prepared from the onions cooked with the leg, passed through a sieve and mixed with a bécha-

85

mel sauce (white milk sauce) and vegetables cut in brunoise (dices) and mushrooms. Re-cover the leg with the same paste and envelop same with a pig's caul, cover with bread-crumbs and brown, garnish with braised lettuces, roast potatoes and peas with mint.

As it is named after him, it is bound to be good ; but really there are limits to one's capacity.

*   *   *   *   *

Isn't that enough about hotels for the time being ? We'll come back to the subject later on. But let's go a-hunting once more among the restaurants. After a series of such meals one is apt to feel rather over-powered by hoteldom : it must be the knee-breeched and top-hatted flunkeys at the Mayfair.

So let's be on our way.

SIMPSON'S, 100, Strand, W.C.2.
(Simpson's Grand Divan Tavern.)

Attend now, all housewives and home-cookers who think they know how to roast a joint.

You think you have been roasting legs of mutton and sirloins of beef in your little two-by-four gas ovens ? Not a bit of it. Nary a piece of meat has been roasted in such ovens. Baked, maybe : roasted, certainly not.

Should this revelation upset you, maybe the follow-ing will cheer you up. I have the recipe for roasting ;

and from no less an authority than Mr. Willis, who is chef at Simpson's. Here you are :

Buy, borrow or build an open fireplace eight feet wide, six feet high and two feet deep (approximate dimensions). This gives a capacity of ninety-six cubic feet. Fill this space with red-hot coals : the finest grade being imported direct from Gehenna. And there's your fire.

In front of this, hang four chains like anchor cables ; from these chains depend hooks stolen from the cranes of building contractors. Underneath them, place a drip-pan ; big enough to float the *Berengaria*.

Thus shall you be able to roast a joint.

If all this seems to be too much for you to do on a wet afternoon, then go to Simpson's instead. Yes ; go thither as so many other thousands of sensible people do, have done and will continue to do for uncountable years, I trust.

Although I have been a frequent visitor to Simpson's, it had never occurred to me that there might be quite a big organization to ensure my getting such excellent roast beef. Simpson's is so pleasantly quiet that the excellence of service becomes a thing taken for granted.

" Want to see over the place ? Of course ! " said Mr. Fred Heck, who is the manager.

" Here is the bar "—he led me to it. " What'll you have ? "

" What'll I . . . ? Oh yes ! Thanks very much ! "

And we did.

From there we went downstairs to that sanctum presided over by the genial, kindly Mr. Willis.

The whole place is as spruce and clean as a brand-new hospital on opening day. Some of the staff downstairs, whose job it is to keep the place clean, don't regard Mr. Willis as being genial and kindly. He sees to it that they do their work.

In the huge refrigerator were saddles of mutton. Rows upon rows of 'em. Mr. Willis said that in the main ice storage they had two hundred saddles. Such a number seems sufficient to cope with any emergency.

A Scotch salmon of 23 lb. had just been " smoked." We tried it. Mr. Heck, Mr. Willis and myself. We formed a resolution forthwith, that if the customers didn't like it, we'd finish the whole salmon ourselves.

Potato washers . . . plate washers . . . live trout . . . huge turbot . . . radishes, radishes, radishes . . . apple pies, each meant for one person . . . such sirloins of beef oozing with gravy . . . cabbage . . . roast potatoes and boiled ones . . . a tremendous show of English cuisine at its very best.

From here, into the " wet " department. Of course, the endless arrays of wine. And also—what pleases Americans so much—rye whisky ; many bottles thereof.

In here are kept the old brass plates that graced the doorway of the original Simpson's.

It made us thirsty to look at all this good stuff ; we thought of poor Mr. Willis standing near that huge, open fire and it occurred to us that maybe he, too, might be thirsty.

. . . after which we all felt better.

Then I had luncheon in an official capacity.

Not before meeting Charlie Brown, the chief carver.

"How long have you been here, Charlie ? " asked Mr. Heck. "It's fifty-one years, isn't it ? "

"Fifty-one ? " Charlie echoed indignantly. "It's fifty-four years next August since I carved my first saddle of mutton at Simpson's. And I'd been carving for two years, before that ! "

By now, he knows something about saddles of mutton. In spite of his seventy-six years of age, Charlie Brown can outcarve most of the younger knife-wielders ; mere youngsters of forty, fifty and sixty or so. He has carved for Their Majesties the King and Queen—by Royal Command. And what the younger carvers must find so annoying is that Brown gets all the attention of the ladies !

By now you will have gathered that saddle of mutton with red-currant jelly is a speciality of the place. So is roast sirloin of beef. When ordering either of these —and also other daily specialities—you pay a fixed price which includes " cabbage, potatoes, Cheddar or Cheshire cheese, etc."

Boiled turbot with lobster sauce, at three-and-six, is a dish at Simpson's of which expatriates speak in hushed whispers.

Just look at the names of these good, old English dishes :

	s.	d.
Kentish chicken pudding . .	4	0
Boiled silverside of salt beef, with carrots and dumplings . .	4	0
Real turtle soup . . .	3	0
Fish and oyster pie . .	3	6
Stewed eels, port wine sauce .	3	6
Jugged hare, port wine sauce .	4	0
Stewed fresh pear and syllabub	1	3
Preserved ginger and cream .	1	3
Grilled plum pudding . .	0	9
Stilton cheese . . .	0	9

A host of other things. The prices are ridiculously low for what you get. For you are served with the best obtainable in the market ; and you get such quantities to eat that it is not advisable to go to Simpson's unless you are really hungry. If you eat yourself into a state of torpor, Palmer-the-cheery, who looks after the dining-rooms upstairs, smiles happily. He has satisfied a customer ; and that is his mission in life.

As to what you can drink—well, Simpson's has as good a selection as anyone. It may be of interest to you to know that in the cellars there are magnums of champagne that looked at Mr. Heck reproachfully as we passed them by. They just long to be poured out and to be drunk by understanding and appreciative people like you. Mr. Heck, however, will say that the best drink is Bass's Number One blended with bitter beer. His advice is worth taking, if you are a beer drinker, for Mr. Heck knows what he is talking about. There is also my favourite Canadian Club whisky. Let it be known too that in the cellars are bottles of a dark sherry worthy of more than casual attention.

Some of the carving wagons which are wheeled from table to table have been in use ever since the opening of the place ; and that, I think, was in 1828. Sometimes an American evinces a desire to have one made to take home ; he changes his mind on learning that the cost would " set him back " about £60. There is a deal of work that goes into the carving (no joke intended), turning and building of one of these mahogany wagons.

Yes : by the way ; in the winter months—those that have a blessed " R " in their names—Simpson's serve steak, kidney, mushroom and oyster pudding. On Thursdays, that is. Be counselled and guided by thousands who make a devout pilgrimage to Simpson's for this dish.

How would you like to try one of their famous

eighteenth-century recipes in your own home? It is certain that Mr. Heck will have no objection to your attempting it; so here are the instructions:

Coventry Pigeon Pie (for four persons).

Two large fat pigeons; 1 lb. tender lean steak; $\frac{1}{2}$ lb. lean cooked bacon. Small quantity chopped onion, mixed herbs, chopped parsley, and pepper and salt. One breakfast-cupful of water.

Method : Beat out the steak into very thin slices, cut pigeons into halves, lay in pie dish with alternate layers of steak and the seasoning and stock and bacon. Cover with a puff pie crust. The halves of pigeons are improved if stuffed with the chopped livers of the birds mixed with a small piece of veal stuffing.

If you don't happen to get it right, there is only one thing for you to do. That is, go to Simpson's; admit your own failure, and ask that Mr. Willis make a Coventry Pigeon Pie for you to eat then and there. Whilst that solution may not tend to restore your self-esteem where cooking is concerned, it will do much to restore your equanimity—and that of the people who were to have eaten your attempt.

On the ground-floor is the main dining-room, reserved for the exclusive use of men only. There's plenty of accommodation for ladies in the two dining-rooms on the first floor. Most attractively decorated, too—so I've been assured. It must be so, for my nerves have never been jarred by the *décors*.

Which makes me think. Simpson's have begun a campaign to appeal to the æsthetic in men's minds. The lavatories, for instance. Usually a utilitarian resort, boasting of nothing startling in the way of decorations. During the recent renovations these places underwent a startling metamorphosis, and emerged as poems in white tile, black marble and bright metal work. The washing of hands becomes a pleasant ritual.

Right next door is the bar of which mention has been made already. Farther along is one of the most comfortable lounges in London. All these are downstairs. On the ground floor, in addition to the men's dining-room, is the cigar stand : you can buy your smokes with one hand, what time you check your hat and coat with the other.

Simpson's is indeed to be congratulated on keeping one dining-room for men only. It forms a pleasant sanctuary permeated with the incense of roast meat, presided over by white-garbed priests and acolytes, who know their jobs and carry them out right well. Maybe they're a bit afraid of Charlie Brown, who presides over this room, looking like a pink-cheeked, benign old High Priest.

So long as Simpson's-in-the-Strand is in existence, then we need have no fear as to the safety of the

Empire. Simpson's is an institution—a reminder—a landmark. Long may it continue to serve the world's best roast beef and saddle of mutton.

BIRCH'S, *Cornhill, E.C.*

Whilst we are on the subject of genuinely English eating-places let's make one of our famous whirlwind tours of some others—having dealt at some length with Simpson's, the established favourite of them all.

There is Birch's in Cornhill; somewhere in the " E.C.s." This is the place that does all the catering for those truly magnificent Aldermanic banquets; those dinners to which our City Fathers waddle with anticipatory gleams in their eyes.

Never have I been fortunate enough to attend one of these functions; being no Alderman; nor a father— of the City ilk. But there can be no doubt as to the excellence of the food provided. Ask a casual question of one who has been to such a banquet; only be prepared to listen for an hour to the highest flights of praise.

Birch's cater daily to scores of men who are " something in the City." Has done for generations, be it noted. The place has altered but little during the last two centuries. There is no jazz band there to destroy the patina of eld which envelops Birch's. Turtle soup, punch, and plain honest English food have made this place famous.

Wars may come : epidemics rage : dynasties be founded and stricken low—but Birch's goes on for ever.

" For which, let us render thanks," say the owners of some of the noblest paunches in the City.

THE CHESHIRE CHEESE, 145, *Fleet Street, E.C.4.*

Even as all devout Mohammedans desire to make the Holy Pilgrimage to Mecca, so do all Americans yearn to visit the Cheshire Cheese. Not Americans only, by a long chalk.

These fanatics wish to sit in Doctor Johnson's chair ; see pictures of Doctor Johnson ; pick up little snippets of information about Doctor Johnson. In a coined word, these pilgrims suffer from "lexicographerphobia."

Still, there's no harm in going to the Cheshire Cheese. Many thousands of people have been. There is quite a large number that goes there regularly as a matter of course. Especially if that " course " happens to be steak-and-kidney pudding.

Around half-past six on Wednesday evening, the Cheshire Cheese is crowded with devout worshippers come to see the darling god of their prayers. A huge steak-and-kidney pudding, wellnigh overflowing the great brown bowl, is brought in and carved with appropriate ceremony due to such a concoction.

The bare fact that this ritual has taken place for a number of years is sufficient to show that the pudding's excellence has been well proven.

With it there is but one thing to drink and that is bitter beer. This drinking of bitter beer must be emphasized thoroughly, for it is part of the traditional pudding-rite of the Cheshire Cheese. Those unfortunate people who happen to dislike this drink are deserving of commiseration.

After this, toasted cheese, sizzling in tin trays. And Cheshire Cheese Punch, from a china bowl. This last item being a drink that appeals to all and sundry of every nationality. What a delicious Punch !

ANDERTON'S HOTEL, *Fleet Street*, E.C.4.

It is so long since I was last here, that my visits have become but memories : vague yet pleasant withal.

A quick yet good and cheap table d'hôte luncheon can be had here.

Straightforward English food. Very English.

FALSTAFF, 70, *Fleet Street*, E.C.4.

Across the road is this haunt so much-beloved of editors, advertising men and others connected with the production of our many newspapers.

Whilst it would be easy enough to pick on the foibles of the gentlemen of the Press, there's no gainsaying that when it comes to eating and drinking, they pick out good places.

The Falstaff is terribly hearty ; overwhelmingly cheerful. There is a Cold Buffet and Snack Counter, groaning beneath a burden of good things to eat. The drinking-bar is kept busy every minute of its operative hours. In using the word " busy " nothing else but " busy " is meant.

You know there's something very thirst-provoking about working in an atmosphere of paper and print. Ask any newspaper man ; ask that cheerful man at the end of the bar there—the one with his bowler hat tipped forward on to the end of his nose.

KING LUD, *Ludgate Circus, E.C.4.*

Welsh rarebits and beer at this public-house.

CHESTERFIELD ARMS, *Mayfair, W.1.*

An amazing instance of London's heterogeneous nature. In the heart of Mayfair—the haunt of These Charming People who wear Green Hats—is this singularly pleasant and charming little hostelry. An inn—no more. Upstairs is an unpretentious dining-room, where you can get a good plainly-cooked meal at a very reasonable price. A table d'hôte dinner costing half a crown.

There are no frills to the Chesterfield Arms. No flowers on the tables are necessary. There are no frills in the cooking either ; but what can you expect for such a low price ? Whatever you may expect, you'll be pleasantly surprised at the Chesterfield Arms.

* * * * *

We will try some other " pubs " later on.

SCOTT'S, 18, *Coventry Street*, *W.*1.

Messieurs et Mesdames! A Paris on trouve le Restaurant Prunier, où on mange les huitres, les homards and a whole lot of other different kinds of shellfish.

Say buddy! you can't tell me a thing about Billy the Oysterman's place in New York. I know it well. Have even managed to eat a dozen Blue Points, clam chowder, broiled live lobster all at one meal. Certainly, Billy the Oysterman's on East 20th Street is well known to me. Also, I know The Lobster on West 45th Street just by Broadway.

Which brings us to Scott's in Coventry Street, London. How does it bring us there? Well, don't you know Scott's? They say in Shanghai, that there is a derelict " old soak " who saves up his money each winter to go to Scott's for a lobster. Unfortunately he gets no farther than the nearest bar . . . and away go his high hopes, resolutions and money.

North Bornean head hunters are convinced that the word " Scott's " is some magic password among white men.

Scott's. That restaurant which has recently " gone modern " enough to install a new cocktail bar and lounge. Certainly, there is no restaurant which has such an atmosphere of distinctive and instinctive good breeding. In all good conscience it should have that atmosphere ; having been founded in the year 1658.

Scott's have Natives—and the recently-bedded Blue Points of America. These are priced at eight and five shillings a dozen respectively. To pay eight shillings a dozen for those exceedingly well-bred oysters from the sea bed of Whitstable would seem expensive at first glance. It must be taken into consideration, however, that Scott's have the pick of England's oyster supply, and the oysters you get there are just so much better than you can get anywhere else in these, our British Isles. The transplanted Blue Point is not so expensive as the native oyster, and many people prefer them, regardless of the price being lower.

An American laughed loud and long on being told that fried oysters would cost him six shillings and sixpence a dozen in London ; thought his " leg was being pulled." He stopped laughing when he took a glance at Scott's menu. Oysters in England are not so plentiful as in the United States of America.

Not to put too fine a point on it, Scott's is an expensive place, but it has the best of all reasons for so being, for at the same time it is exceedingly good. Only the best of shellfish can hope to appear at this restaurant. Unless a prawn both is and looks to be worth the money, it cannot hope to be sold at Scott's for fourpence. Very likely one prawn would cost more than that ; four shillings per dozen is the price on the menu.

Do you like Bisque d'Homard—that is, Lobster

Soup—such as you dream of? Scott's, and only Scott's, have got it to perfection. To the tune of three shillings a time, and worth every ha'penny of the price.

All those wonderful things like Lobster Thermidor; Crab Salad—guaranteed to engender the finest selection of nightmares; Quail; Pigeon; Porterhouse Steak; and Roast Duck and Apple Sauce at sixteen shillings a bird. Go to Scott's for them.

Then if you like stewed fruit, Scott's recommend rhubarb. At least, it is to be supposed they do; for it is written in French and in big, black type on the menu!

A mere apple or orange costs ninepence.

Before starting out for a meal at this excellent restaurant, disabuse yourself of the notion that you can put a ten-shilling note into your pocket and have a slap-up dinner for two at this restaurant. For ten shillings one of you could have a very simple meal and tip the waiter more or less adequately; the other would have to drink ice water.

Yet if you patronize Scott's, knowing the place to be expensive, you can be sure of enjoying the best food in the world of its kind, cooked and served as it should be. Always. There's a pleasantness appertaining to this restaurant; a " je ne sais quoi " that is the envy of its cheaper and less successful rivals.

Scott's is as good in the question of drinkables as

they are in eatables. If you choose, you can have a red or a white wine by the carafe or half carafe—this costs four shillings for the former and half a crown for the half-size.

If you dine upstairs, ask for Petersen, who is head waiter. He'll minister to you and fuss over you nicely, as though you were the one person he had been hoping to see.

Scott's has specialities for each day and here they are :

MONDAY.
Roast Sirloin of Beef and
Yorkshire Pudding.

TUESDAY.
Roast Saddle of Mutton and
Red Currant Jelly.

WEDNESDAY.
Steak and Kidney Pudding.

THURSDAY.
Stewed Lamb and Peas.

FRIDAY.
Grilled Salmon and Cucumber.

SATURDAY.
Minced Chicken and Poached Egg.

Should it interest you, you can buy things from Scott's to take home with you. A great boon to many.

Turtle soup at 10s. 6d. a pint : smoked salmon at
12s. 6d. per lb.

Having mentioned the fact that Scott's is an expensive restaurant, it is only fair and right to show cause.
The best way is by advising you to read carefully these
two recipes. When you consider that sole prepared
thusly costs but a beggarly three shillings and sixpence,
why you are almost tempted to pay double through
pity for Scott's.

Sole à la Scott's.

Braise a sole (or fillets) in a little fish stock and
white wine in equal parts. Remove sole (or fillets)
as soon as cooked. Simmer stock on moderate heat,
adding cream and later a little butter. Slice three
or four medium-sized white mushrooms, cook in
butter in sauté pan, add about one dozen shrimps
or four or five prawns and three or four oysters, cook
for six or seven minutes. Place the sole (or fillets)
on a dish and decorate round edge of dish with
Pomme Duchesse. Arrange the mushrooms and
shrimps (or prawns or oysters) as garniture over the
fish (sole or fillets), add the prepared stock and finish
by letting the whole take a light brown glaze in the
oven or under a salamander.

Homard Thermidor.

Boil a live lobster for twenty-five minutes, remove
from water and split the lobster in half. Put both

shells aside. Cut the lobster into small pieces, next take some chopped shallots and parsley and simmer gently in equal quantities of fish stock and white wine for fifteen minutes. Add to this a little English mustard mixed in cold water, add white wine sauce for desired quantity, also a little cream and then butter. Place the scallops of lobster in the two shells. Finish edge of shells by decorating with a little Pomme Duchesse. Pour the sauce over the lobster and brown nicely in a hot oven or under a salamander.

Lobster Thermidor is one of my greater delights. Scott's have benefited muchly by my yielding to the indulgence of my desires. Assuredly there is no better Lobster Thermidor to be found in any restaurant. No : not even at Prunier's.

Scott's is one of those few restaurants to which one can go again and again and never feel bored or disappointed with the food.

LYONS & CO., LTD.

" Let's go to Lyons " is the deuce of a good slogan. It covereth such a multitude of restaurants too.

For instance, if you think you will splash a bit and decide to go to the Trocadero for tea, Lyons' directors rub their hands gleefully. Or maybe you'd like to do the odd spot of dancing at the Empress Rooms. There will be more washing of hands with invisible soap. All Lyons.

That's why it is advisable to treat Lyons with a considerable amount of care and detail. It's too big an institution to be disposed of in a page or two. After all, an organization that enables you to buy a cup of tea for twopence, or a supper for yourself alone to the tune of £1 7s. 9d. counting nothing for drinks, couvert or tips, is deserving of our closest attention.

So we will take Les Chez Lyons to pieces—figuratively.

The tea-shops first of all. Those white-paint and gilt establishments you see all over the place. Whilst you may have a feeling of antipathy toward them, there's no gainsaying that these tea-shops fulfil a definite purpose.

Here are three items taken from a Lyons tea-shop menu : Yorkshire Pudding, 1d. ; Custard Powder Sauce, 1d. extra ; " Try Buzz with your tea or coffee daily, 1d. extra." When I order roast beef, I like to think the Yorkshire pudding comes with it—either automatically or by the Grace of God. Nothing of the kind at a Lyons tea-shop, however ; it's one penny extra. As for custard powder sauce . . . the frankness of such an admission is deserving of the highest praise. And what is " Buzz " ? There's nothing on the menu that gives you any clue to its identity. Try

Buzz ! The waitress will tell you that it's a kind of chocolate biscuit.

There's no doubt but that the iniquitous habit developed by people in offices, of going out for a cup of coffee at eleven in the morning, is why Messrs. J. Lyons & Co., Ltd., have attained a staggeringly huge daily service of over four hundred thousand cups of coffee. Are my rough mathematics correct in assuming that this quantity would fill a reservoir of 12,500 gallons capacity ? Quite a respectable swimming-bath.

Let's go from the tea-shops and visit one of those gigantic marble palaces known as Corner Houses. For our purpose, we'll inspect the Oxford Street Corner House, which though not the biggest is yet the most modern. What this place cost to build I don't know, but it is obvious to the most untutored that the total expense must have been colossal. Yet, in spite of all its magnificence, in spite of the marble pictures which are really beautiful, in spite of the ten tons of " Staybrite " metal used, you can still buy a solitary cup of tea for $2\frac{1}{2}d$.

If you want to go really gay you can order things with French names ; such as *omelette aux champignons*, or *méringue Chantilly*. But " *fish au gratin* " sounds rather mysterious. I like to be able to greet a seabeast by name when it's put before me. " Gendarme herring " has a certain appeal. It has that spick-and-span appearance of the smart Swiss policeman. . . .

Lights, colour, decorations, service and music : all can be yours for the modest sum needed to buy a cup of tea, and that, too, is included in the price !

Really, Lyons is a wonderful place.

Take the Popular Café in Piccadilly.

You can dance here afternoon and evening. You can listen to music, and generally some vocalist is engaged for the delectation of the patrons. Most certainly you can eat ; choosing your food from a menu that is far more French than the Corner House one.

Even like Gennaro's, this restaurant has different specialities each day. You may thank heaven if you are lucky enough to choose a " boiled leg of pork and pease pudding " day ; it being one of the most characteristic of Olde Englishe dishes.

Alas ! There is no mention of a cup of tea at $2\frac{1}{2}d$. on this menu. We have gotten to a more rarefied plane ; no cups of tea. But you can get " Braised York ham and céleri." There is a pleasant dash of Continental swagger about that " céleri." Perhaps one of the best things of the Popular Café is the 2s. 3d. table d'hôte luncheon, a specimen of which I reproduce for your amusement and edification. Certainly, there can be no complaint on the score of value for money. There are courses enough and plenty of choice in each for the beggarly two shillings and threepence to suit the most niggardly-minded of people.

MENU.

Hors-d'Œuvres.   Grape Fruit.
Smoked Herring.   Salami.
Clear Jardinière.
Leek and Potato Soup.

———

Fried Sprats and Lemon.
Fresh Haddock, Egg Sauce.

———

Jugged Hare Bourguignonne.
Haricot Ox Tail.
Roast Lamb and Mint Sauce.
Sprouts.   Roast Potatoes.

———

Lemon Pudding.   Vanilla Ice.

———

Cheese.
Apple.   Banana.   Orange.
2s. 3d.

From here it is no distance at all to the Coventry Street Corner House : the biggest of all these mammoth bun-parlours. Heaven knows how many thousands of people can be seated here : I certainly have no idea. There are generally three orchestras on different floors. A Café de Petit Repas open day and night ; a Sun Vita Café where one gets Soda Fountain specialities ; hairdressing shops ; wine and spirit counters ; flowers ; chocolates ; cakes ; candy ; cigarettes ; delicatessen and grocery counters—and a theatre ticket office. Which seems to cover the ground of modern, everyday requirements.

In addition, there is quite a pleasant cocktail lounge called " L'Apéritif."

The same food—much the same noise—the same people come here as patronize other Lyons Corner Houses.

Downstairs, it is known as the Gorgonzola Room ; owing to the green veining on the marble walls.

The Strand Corner House, also open day and night, is much the same kind of place though not on such a large scale.

So we come to the Trocadero—which is J. Lyons & Co.'s excursion into the field of expensive catering ; though still to the masses. It's the kind of place where coffee goes through a form of transmutation and becomes " Café Moka, 9d."

Not so very long ago I used to invite myself to tea in the Empire Room, Trocadero. For the good reason that in here one got the very best tea in the world. Delicious sandwiches, toasted buns, a selection of cakes that made choosing quite a pastime, tea, coffee or chocolate to perfection.

Now the same idea is carried on, though in another part of the Trocadero. For me, it is not the same thing. Another port of call to be struck from my list.

It's in the Grill Room, however, that all the fun and gaiety are centred. Just look around at the decorations. Lyons are mighty proud of their latest efforts, and will produce all manner of figures and facts about them.

As to whether or no you like these modern décors—

it is entirely a matter of personal choice. For what these decorations purport to be, they are excellent.

Mr. Cochran—yes, the one and only and inimitable " C. B."—puts on a Supper Show. The show varies somewhat. A few, pretty good cabaret turns ; and of course " Mr. Cochran's Young Ladies." It only remains for some theatrical producer to form a chorus of nothing but titled cuties and the pinnacle of theatrical snobbery will have been achieved. Of course chorus girls are ladies : is it necessary to bill them as such ?

There is also a band here. You will do well to sit as far away as it is possible ; and that is really a considerable distance, for it is as well that you should understand that the Grill Room is a very large place indeed.

Using me as a relay-race baton, I was passed along from " commis " to wine waiter ; from wine waiter to section head waiter ; from section head waiter to chief head waiter and so finally into the Presence of Monsieur Monbiot who is *maître d'hôtel*.

" You must have a drink," he said, observing my state of exhaustion.

" Thank you," I murmured. " M. Monbiot, you are an artist in two senses of the word, I understand."

His chest expanded. " True, true ! "

" Your etchings have been praised by people competent to judge. Myself, I admire them tremendously, but cannot afford to buy them. . . ."

A hopeful pause ; but nothing happened.

" So I want your expert counsel in the matter of food. Of sweets, desserts, entremets, dolce, mehl-speisen—whichever language you like to use."

" Ha! Yes! What shall I tell you? "

" Two recipes, please," I begged, coming straight to the point.

" Ah Marjorie! " he whispered.

Uncomfortably I wriggled in my chair—pity that I was in the presence of a broken heart and not knowing quite what to do about it.

" Yes, here is one! " He turned to me beamingly. " It is called Soufflé Glacé Marjorie. You see the price on the menu is five shillings and sixpence. But it's worth much more—for it is a work of art like my etchings. You say you admire them? "

" Very much. But I can't afford . . ."

" Good! Here is the recipe! "

Soufflé Glacé Marjorie.

Appareil of iced biscuits with essence of vanilla and strawberry. Freeze in a mould (high) and after $1\frac{1}{4}$ hours empty its contents. Put same on to a piece of rounded Génoise cake, envelop the whole with a mixture of a light Italian meringue (6 whites of eggs and $\frac{1}{2}$ lb. sugar). Powder the finished piece with vanilla sugar, put quickly into the oven and proceed the same as with Soufflé Surprise.

Serve Cherries Jubilé with Kirsch separate.

" And here is another one. Write it down ! "

In the presence of such imperiousness what was there for me to do, but write it down ?

I did.

Appareil of Iced Biscuit.

Seven yolks of eggs, one quartern of syrup at 27° whipped on a low fire to give the mixture body ; allow it to cool, add about ½ pint meringue mixture, of cooked butter and 1 pint of whipped cream, form two flavours—vanilla and strawberry.

Cerises Jubilé

One quartern of syrup at 25°, two tablespoons of red-currant jelly ; melt this and add 1 quartern of Kirsch and 250 grammes of cherries, fresh or bottled. Serve hot.

" And here is a veal recipe. I had it for luncheon yesterday ! " M. Monbiot continued, having got into his stride.

Escaloppe de Veau Charbonnière.

Escallops passed in flour, eggs and bread-crumbs, and fried in butter. Strips of mushrooms, egg plant and truffles fried in butter placed on top of the escallop, with a few capers. Just a little gravy round the dish, and then melted butter and chopped parsley. (4s.)

" And now you must have another drink ! You say you like my etchings ? "

" Exceedingly ! "

" Ah ! You must have a big drink ! "

*   *   *   *   *

Undoubtedly the Trocadero offers the most astounding value for money. Under the guidance of such as Monsieur Monbiot there could be nothing less than a superb cuisine.

It's the immensity of the place ; the flocks of waiters ; the paying at a desk as you go out ; the decorations—which are so impressive as to reduce first-time customers to a state of speechless awe and amazement : in the Grill Room one feels so inconspicuous and unimportant—but that feeling soon wears off. Deft service from waiters who know how to smile even at rush times, soon dispels the discomfort first induced by the outsize dimensions of the place.

You can get a five-course table d'hôte dinner in the Grill Room for four shillings. You can get an à la carte luncheon in the Restaurant du Soleil for £2 9s. just for one. Neither of these prices represents the lowest or the highest you can pay ; neither of them includes drinks or tips, naturally.

These prices are quoted to you, however, to show you how Messrs. Lyons cater to all pockets—even at the Trocadero.

" Let's go to Lyons."

REGENT PALACE HOTEL, *Piccadilly Circus, W.1.*

Of course, this place is a Lyons. It reeks of Lyons in every corner of the building. Not that that is anything against it ; on the contrary, it's a guarantee of service and value.

It is, I believe, the largest hotel in Europe—from the viewpoint of guest accommodation. In shape it is like an iron : one of those instruments used for putting scorch marks on shirts and handkerchiefs. The apex of the Regent Palace points to Piccadilly Circus ; once alleged to be the forcing-ground of sin, vice, crime and depravity. Talking of such things, the Regent Palace also had a quite undeserved reputation for being naughty : earned during War years. House detectives, floor superintendents, housekeepers and other " snoops " are so abundant that it is a real difficulty to make a date here with a pretty girl and not be suspect of the most nefarious designs.

On the ground-floor of this residential Lyons is the famous Rotunda Café. Famous for being a meeting-place of exiles returned from God knows what faraway corners of the earth. Famous for that farcical ritual that takes place when you order an alcoholic drink : " Are you staying here, sir ? " Famous for being a haunch-repository for that strange genus of woman whose husband is vaguely " somewhere abroad." That explanation being an alibi, first for sitting in the

Rotunda Café drinking " Gin and It " ; secondly—
should a chance pick-up acquaintanceship progress thus
far—an alibi for long-lost maidenhood. Be it noted :
I speak not from personal experience. No. When I
gather peaches, I like them to have reached a certain
maturity : not past it.

There is a restaurant here which serves a truly
astounding table d'hôte for 2s. 3d. Look at this
specimen menu and judge for yourself.

Hors-d'Œuvre

or

Grape Fruit en Coupe

or

Crème Santé.

———

Filet de Bar Frit Orly

or

Curry d'Œuf Madras.

———

Pied de Veau Portugaise

or

Steak and Kidney Pie

or

Roast Pork Sauce Reinette

Panais à la Crème

Pommes Mousseline.

———

Baked Apple

or

Glace à l'Orange

or

Fruits Frais.

And what about this dinner at three shillings and sixpence ?

Hors-d'Œuvre Lucullus.
Barquette de Caviar.
Saumon Fumé.
Grape Fruit en Coupe.

———

Consommé Paysanne.
Crème Derby.

———

Suprême de Flétan Tout-Paris
ou
Filet de Plie Frit Sauce Tartare.

———

Noisette d'Agneau Anversoise
ou
Jambon Braisé Florentine.
Pommes Berny.

———

Poulet Rôti en Broche.
Salade Gauloise.

———

Coupe Bohémienne
ou
Regent Wonder Cake.
Friandises.

Now that you have gazed in admiration upon these two menus, take a little trip to the Grill Room, which is way downstairs. Two flights : the first flight being punctuated by the gentlemen's cloakroom and the second flight by the ladies' likewise. Store away that information for when you bring your friends hither.

The Grill Room is a large, more-or-less-square room with too many pillars, seemingly too many waitresses, and far too much noise.

Smile benevolently at the *maître d'hôtel* who advances to conduct you to that discreet little table for two, away from the orchestra. Smile, and as he strides pompously, looking neither to right nor left, pick out your own location. For that " discreet little table for two, away from the orchestra " is right by the service door ; and you know what that means, don't you ? Artful dogs, those Grill Room head waiters, but they should not catch you twice with the same cooing siren song.

It's all à la carte here except the music as dispersed, or disbursed, by the orchestra ; and that is terribly table d'hôte.

The Regent Palace does not pretend to compete with the Grill Room of its swankier brother, the Trocadero. Nevertheless, the food is really eatable and, at the price, extremely good value.

On the menu there is a choice of twenty-five different dishes in the fish line. There are forty-two sweets ; and thirteen different iced desserts.

A choice of three *plats du jour*, such as Oxtail Bourgeoise at one shilling and fivepence ; Best End of Lamb Sarladaise at one-and-nine, and at that same price Braised Ham, Spinach and Potato Croquettes. In addition, there is a Plat Special, such as La Poulet

Sauté Maryland at three shillings. The French alone is worth the extra money.

Every Wednesday there are Special Indian Curries. Every day a choice of two hot joints such as Roast Ribs of Beef and Yorkshire Pudding at one shilling and twopence ; or Boiled Leg of Mutton, Mashed Turnips and Caper Sauce at one-and-eight.

These things are all additional to the large à la carte menu : so you ought to find something you like. Certainly the prices shouldn't bother you, as they are all on a par with those quoted.

You can dance in the Grill Room. Here is the time-table—or whatever such schedules may be called.

THE SALON DE DANSE
In the Grill Room.

Daily (Except Sunday)—
DANCE TEA . . . . . . 1s. 6d.
(Saturday, 2s. 6d.) 3.45 to 5.45.
SUPPER DANCE . . . . . 3s. 6d.
9.30 to 12.30.
(Saturday, 4s. 6d.) 9.30 to 12 midnight.

Sunday—
DANCE TEA . . . . . . 2s. 6d.
3.45 to 5.45.
DINNER DANCE . . . . . 4s. 6d.
7.15 to 11 p.m.

These prices include tea, supper and dinner respectively. Here is a typical supper menu :

117

Hors-d'Œuvre.
Barquette de Caviar.
Grape Fruit. Saumon Fumé.

———

Consommé Double en Tasse
ou
Consommé au Curry.

———

Coquille de Crevettes Bercy
ou
Filet de Plaice Frit Sauce Tartare.

———

Chipolata Grillé au Lard
ou
Poulet Américaine
ou
Œufs Brouillés aux Champignons
ou

BUFFET FROID.
Jambon à la Gelée.
Langue Ecarlate.
Bœuf rôti.
Salade.

———

Canapé Écossais
ou
Coupe Bohémienne.
Frivolités.

When you consider that you get all this and three
hours of dance music to which you may cavort and
gambol for an inclusive charge of three shillings and
sixpence, you'll agree that Lyons really " do you

proud." If you still feel disgruntled and that you are not getting value for money, then " gang awa hame " to your granite and your Grampians. You have no right to be in London.

By way of an à la carte luncheon suggestion try a chump chop with braised onion, followed by green figs and cream. A strange meal, yet one of singular excellence.

LEGRAIN'S, *Gerrard Street*, *W*.1.

'Twas but recently that I had celebrated my ninth birthday when my father first took me to Legrain's coffee shop. It would be tactless to say how many years ago that is ; for Mrs. Compton Mackenzie was honouring us with her company. I adored her in a silent and gulping manner. Nine years old. Early loves are hard to forget. . . .

Legrain's blend, roast and grind coffee for sale to the public. They have a shop devoted to this purpose. Another part of their premises consists of a café bar, where one sits at tables and drinks coffee as made by the delightful woman behind the urns of boiling water. The coffee is " dripped " into glasses. If you wish, you can buy digestive biscuits to nibble with your coffee ; cigarettes to smoke with your coffee. But that concludes the list of things you can buy.

Coffee is the first, second and all the thoughts of

people who go to Legrain's. Such coffee it is, too : for this bar is Legrain's advertisement.

There's nothing ornate. Simple tables having deep red-tile tops ; plain bentwood chairs, and there you are. A couple of waitresses take orders, transmitting it to the woman who must have brewed incalculable glasses of coffee—every glassful a model of excellent French coffee.

Writers and actors come here. So do business men ; and clinch the deals that " hung fire " due to a disappointing luncheon. They can be certain that there will be no slip up in the coffee. So do scores of people for no reason other than that they like coffee as it should be made—to drink it in an atmosphere fragrant with the scent of roasting coffee beans. So will you become an ardent habitué of Legrain's when once you have been there. That is, if you are particular about your coffee—as I'm sure you must be, to have read as far as this.

VEERASAWMY'S INDIA RESTAURANT,
99, *Regent Street*, *W*.1.

It is a polite fiction to assume that the Chinese, as a race, are inscrutable. Take a course in reading detective stories, and you'll have proof of that assertion. Nothing is farther from the truth, however. A group of seven Chinese of mixed sexes can make twice as much emotional, facial and verbal babel as any similar group of any other nationality. Go to Chinatown in any big city and prove that for yourselves.

The nearest to inscrutability that I have found in peoples, is that of our blubber-eating brothers, the Esquimaux : a few days in their company and you realize that their inscrutability is just the logical result of racial stupidity. The kayak-paddling boy friend has a low-geared mentality.

Which brings me to Indians. And by Indians I mean the inhabitants of that large peninsula somewhat East of Suez. Not—as our transatlantic friends may first think—the Navajoes, the Sioux, the Iroquois and other Indians of North America.

Veerasawmy's India Restaurant is the worthy representative of Hindustan in London. For here you are met with the nearest thing to inscrutability that one can encounter in many a long day's march. Yet, actually, it is a smiling, courteous, extremely self-possessed dignity. The very essence of instinctive good manners.

This restaurant started as an exhibit at the British Empire Exhibition of 1924 ; after which it was transferred lock, stock and barrel of rice to 99, Regent Street. In May 1930 Doctor I. G. de Zilva bought the place and now runs it as a profitable hobby—being " himself an expert gourmet of the Indian and Eastern dishes."

Running a restaurant is indeed what I call a sensible hobby. How much more pleasantly profitable for everyone, than a hobby that calls for sticking pins through bugs, beetles and butterflies ; or littering a house with chunks of geological specimens.

Food is a hobby worthy of an intelligent man's attention. And that certainly applies to the very charming Dr. de Zilva.

Veerasawmy's is an example of one of London's practical jokes. The address is 99, Regent Street ; that doesn't mean anything, for the entrance to the restaurant is in Swallow Street, two or three doors from our Spanish señorita, Martinez's Restaurant.

The moment you pass through the revolving door you are in a different world. There's not a sound of traffic from the hurly-burly of Regent Street. An oasis of peace, this restaurant. You are greeted by the smiling, white-clad beturbaned doorman who gives you that Oriental salute of two fingers which appears to be so nearly a rude gesture. The *maître d'hôtel*, also in white, appears from nowhere with a delightfully welcoming smile lighting his dark features. You wish to lunch upstairs or down ? If down, which is on the ground floor, you are in a large, airy room having no visible means of ventilation. You don't look out on to any London streetscape. The furnishings are Eastern : bazaar without being bizarre.

Upstairs is my choice, with a table overlooking Regent Street's hushed traffic. Not a sound of it comes through the double windows.

Dr. de Zilva decreed silence ; and he has achieved it.

Of course, now that you are here, you eat curry. It's a good thing if you like it, for, being an Indian restaurant, curries are the *pièce de résistance*. You can get all manner of things, even grilled lamb chops and boiled potatoes, at this place : but why should you eat such ? This is Veerasawmy's and curry is the thing. The Eastern way of reversing certain things being somewhat easier on occasions, it behoves one to give you full warning of the numerous accessories you get with the curry ; then describe the dish itself.

Poppadums. These are feathery puffed biscuits, salty in flavour.

Bombay Duck. A most difficult thing to describe. It resembles nothing so much as the finniest part of a herring that's been kept too long ; then fried in oil too long ; then baked to a crisp. In spite of this unflattering description, Bombay Duck is perfectly palatable ; though, an " acquired taste " shall we say ?

Mango pickle, and mango sweet chutney.

Onion Achar.

Onion Kachumar.

Coco-nut Sambal.

Lime Pickle. This is the one that takes the hair off the back of your neck, if you don't eat it in microscopic quantities. It's the hottest thing invented ; makes a fiery curry seem as mild as ice-cream in comparison.

The curry to have is Madras Chicken. Here is the recipe as written out for me, by Mr. A. H. Beg, who is aide-de-camp to the doctor:

Madras Chicken.
- (*a*) (1) Fry cut onions, garlic and green ginger in butter; when brown, put curry powder.
  (2) Chicken cut into halves.
- (*b*) Fry (1) and (2) on a small gas when turning tender.
- (*c*) Put specially prepared mixture of turmeric juice, lime juice, and tomato paste, and then let it cook till the chicken is fully cooked.

Do you have to be told that a positive Mont Blanc of rice goes with this? Is it any wonder therefore that to order " a curry " is on a par with saying " bring me food for two hungry elephants " ?

As the Indians have an infinite capacity for taking pains with their cooking, it won't come amiss to you to give a couple more Indian recipes. Thanks to the activities of one Mahatma Gandhi everyone has become aware of India. Here's a golden chance for you to learn some of those excellent dishes that the Mahatma denies to himself.

Shanie Kabal (for two).
Take a pound of tender meat (fillet steak). Mince it, and ground it to a fine paste and then put

"Lanka" Brand Kabal Mixture in it and mix it well, and then make it into small round cake shape, and then fry it in butter and serve with fine-cut onions and a piece of lemon.

Now try this "Pillow Rice":

Pillow Rice (for two persons).

Take ½ lb. Pillow Rice (a special rice which has a natural aroma of its own), soak it well in water for about two hours.

Cut a small onion, and 1 lb. butter, fry the onion in butter; when turning brown, put a few whole clove and cardamon, and also cinnamon bark, two or three small pieces, and then the soaked rice. Fry all these on a slow fire; when the rice is getting soft, put hot water just to cover the rice and let it simmer on a gentle heat till the rice is soft, then put saffron water and stir it a minute or two and then leave on the slow fire for a few minutes.

As a dessert you might try a Coupe Jacques of Indian fruits. Certainly it is an experience you won't forget; though it is doubtful if at first you will care very much for the strange flavours. Few people do. However, the curry is such a meal in itself that the majority of folk go straight from curry to coffee. It is worth while having an Indian soup to start your meal.

It is an indisputable fact that any nation having a large peasant population produces excellent soups. Russia gave us Bortsch ; Italy, the Minestrone ; England, nothing at all.

When it comes to the question of suggesting drinks it is hard to advise you. Poulier, *maître d'hôtel* of Veerasawmy's, gives me to understand that there is no hard and fast rule. Beer, lager, spirits, white or red wine—just anything that appeals to the curry-guzzler at the moment.

You'll like Veerasawmy's Restaurant. Everyone, from Dr. de Zilva to the most junior of waiters, is cheerful, quiet and anxious to help you in a wise selection.

The prices generally are most reasonable. For you do get a tremendous amount for your money. You know how rice makes you feel, if you eat a lot of it. Then there's the curry ; and Poppadums . . . and Bombay Duck . . . and, oh heavens ! all those other things.

*　　*　　*　　*　　*

In addition to Veerasawmy's, there are at least a score of Indian restaurants in London.

Unfortunately, there are but few English who are not too Occidental to appreciate the smells that come from the average Oriental kitchen. Cannot stand them, in fact. Though they might feel differently were they in the East.

126

It's not a bad plan, however, to give you the address of another Indian Restaurant. So here it is. *Shafi*, in Gerrard Street. Go try it ; it is very reasonable and good, with quite a different cachet from Veerasawmy's.

EIFFEL TOWER RESTAURANT,
Charlotte Street, W.1.

This place is in a street in that shabby tangle of thoroughfares that lies in the angle between Oxford Street and Tottenham Court Road. Not too savoury.

The Eiffel Tower is very famous ; very strange ; very expensive. The first and third are due to the second—and it is strange on account of its clientèle. The patrons are chiefly practitioners of the arts : those who can afford to pay high prices for exquisite food and good wines. Stulig, who is the proprietor, must have a well-feathered nest by now ; or at least he ought to have, though there may be some doubt about it. For Stulig, who should be hard-boiled, has a strangely tender heart for the strugglers in the artistic world, and has helped many to get established.

I call to mind one supper party given by that eccentric genius, the late Avery Hopwood. Other than my very unimportant self, there was Kay Laurel—also dead, alas !—Dorothy Dickson, two young actors, Epstein and his then-model, a strange chorus boy, startling with his effeminate mannerisms, and a gruff Society columnist. What a mixed bunch ! Celebrating the successful opening of a new show of Avery Hopwood.

At near-by tables, were Cyril Hughes Hartmann, an author of historical novels, with his wife ; Augustus John, representing the painting fraternity ; Tallulah Bankhead with a large party of stagy friends ; a well-known financier now occupied in pursuits to benefit His Majesty the King—a smattering of nondescripts and the like.

The room was full of what would be described as " vivid personalities." Yet not one of them was dominant. For Stulig has impressed the Eiffel Tower so heavily with his own character, that mere patrons can do no more than shed a feeble light to accentuate the greater effulgence of his own.

Without doubt, the cooking here is excellent. But really, M. Stulig ! Has no word reached you of the Great Depression ? Reduce your prices, so that I may return to the fold once more. And a thousand others, placed in similar straits to myself.

THE WORLD'S END CAFÉ, *Cobham*, *Surrey*.

One of these days when the sun shines and there is no immediate prospect of rain, let's go a short distance out of London for tea. To Cobham in Surrey ; which is either seventeen, eighteen or twenty miles from London, according to which signpost you prefer to believe.

Now this village is strung along the main road to Portsmouth ; which means a day-long helter-skelter of traffic. It also means tea-shoppes, filling-stations and other impedimenta of semi-rural, semi-urban, modern, motoring life.

There is this, however. The present-day motorist is not content with a jaunt of a mere seventeen, eighteen or twenty miles—according to the dictates of his personal choice in signposts. When he goes out, he likes to " go places " much farther away than that ; even with petrol at its fantastically high price. So much the better. For what is his loss is your gain ; at least, it will be when I've divulged this secret.

If you have no car, and your automobile-possessing friends appear singularly obtuse to your flagrant hints, then thumb your nose at them and take a Green Line Motor Coach from the Poland Street depot ; the coaches run every fifteen minutes or so ; and make the trip to Cobham in about an hour—the return fare being two shillings and sixpence.

The coach stops at the famous hostelry called the White Lion in Cobham. An hotel known better to thousands upon thousands of motorists than to myself. I mislike me of the people who make calls at wayside inns to drink and merrymake. Mere snobbish prejudice on my part.

Well, having descended from the coach you will see on your left a bright and sparkling array of tastefully assorted petrol pumps. These form the outward and visible sign to the establishment of Thompson & Taylor who redesigned and reconstructed Sir Malcolm Campbell's " Bluebird " ; and you don't need anyone to tell you about that motor-car.

Again slightly to the left of Thompson & Taylor's, is an inconspicuous and rough little lane, by the side of which is a notice-board announcing The World's End Café, " dainty teas in a XVth century cottage." A sign calculated to daunt the stoutest heart. Don't be daunted.

Walk along this lane—or park your car therein—for it is a scant twenty yards in length, ending at the World's End Café.

What a dream place this is.

A garden such as one longs to own. Not formal; not all " cottagey " for the benefit of the tea-bibbing tourists ; but a garden such as you and I would wish to have. A friendly, cheerful garden of friendly cheerful flowers, fruit trees, a lawn, flagged walks, lavender hedge, rosemary. Somewhat at the back a hen run, from which come those inane henny noises portending egg-laying achievements.

In the fields on the other side of the fence. One of them is the ground of the Cobham Village Cricket Club. White-flannelled players . . . the sound of bat meeting ball . . . big shady elm trees . . . a few people lazily watching England's most English pastime.

In another field, velvet-nosed, limpid-eyed Jersey cows being bullied by Alice and Percy—pet goose and gander.

On the flagstones in front of the World's End Café you may meet Flickers—who is a snoozy old cocker spaniel, rich in years, and much too broad in the beam for elegance.

It's a fine day and before going into the cottage we will have our tea on the lawn. Under a striped umbrella, which should look incongruous in this peaceful English setting yet does not.

At the sound of tea-things, Flickers will arouse from her spanielistic meditations and galumph madly to the table in bright anticipation of a lump of sugar— maybe two. That is the main cause for her being so broad in the beam. To win the esteem of the café's owner, you will resist the look of pleading in Flickers's eyes. No sugar.

Sitting thus calls for no desire of conversation. Curiously muffled, for it is quite near, comes the traffic noise of the main road. It blends in with the sound of cows blowing through wide nostrils as they munch the grass : the most delectable grass always grows between fence palings, apparently. Percy the gander decides that he wants a space of forty yards around unoccupied by cows, chickens, or other live stock, and with neck outstretched proceeds to " clear decks," swearing horribly in a raucous, beery tone.

The scent of wallflowers, lilac, and an occasional drift

from the rosemary bush come to colour your thoughts with longings for peace. A contentment steals into the heart. It is relaxing to the mind to drink in the serenity of the scene; drink it through all the senses.

Allied to this balm for the soul, soporific to the brain, comes food for the inner man that is worthy to be classed equally with the beauty of the World's End Cottage, and its garden. No higher praise than that.

The scones, home-made, are perfections of lightness and delicacy. Cream cake, King's cake, flap-jacks, all made under that fifteenth-century roof. All excellent. Yet never bearing that too-oft-met-with stamp of the amateur. They seem to be the products of loving care. The proprietress takes justifiable pride in her handiwork; in her cottage which is " spicker and spanner " than any pin; in her garden, wherein one may find peace and the glory that is England.

Tea of Ceylon growth, specially sent hither from that far-away island of Kandi, pearls and temple girls.

All the cups and plates and so forth are attractive. There is nowhere an effort—a striving after rusticity. The whole place and all to do with it is natural.

It may interest you to know that the café is open from 9 a.m. until 10 p.m. seven days of the week; fifty-two weeks of the year. If you choose you can have a light luncheon or supper inside by the huge open fireplace, wherein is a peat fire to give another heart-bemusing scent to the air.

When inside the café, look at the floor-boards. Did you ever see such broad ones? Reminder of the spacious days, when men thought spaciously and builders were craftsmen—not rent-book carriers.

Don't think you can win Flickers's heart by giving her a lump of sugar—you can't. She merely regards each lump given her as a perquisite peculiarly her own. Her affections are centred entirely upon her mistress.

Having been over to the World's End Café, it would be quite unnecessary to ask if you will go again. The place is a magnet; the force of which can be summed up in one word: charm.

DORCHESTER HOTEL, *Park Lane, W.1.*

It's time that we thought of browsing with the *haut monde* once more. To some slight extent, at least. Otherwise, we may forget how to tie a white tie, and you, oh Lady Fair, will pout with annoyance at being unable to display that latest creation from the House of Norman Hartnell.

So let's pretend we are having the very deuce of a good time; let's go places and do things. Resplendent as to garb and with nice, tidy, open minds we will fare forth.

The imposing edifice that gives the " cold shoulder " to Hyde Park is London's latest and most magnificent example of hotels. None less than the Dorchester.

To many people it will be a source of lasting joy for the grand manner in which valuable ground space in front has been dedicated to nothing more useful than grass, a piece of statuary and a fountain. That's the way to do things ; to show a careless disregard for the possibility of additional income from additional rooms that might have been built on this plot. Use it for grass ; and ignore the wide, open spaces of Hyde Park barely thirty-six feet away.

This is a very grand hotel and very expensive. It is still so new as yet, that there are people who feel a strong desire to throw lighted matches on to the carpets and chairs to burn little holes in everything and give the place a more " matey " look.

It is sad to contemplate upon the probable fate of the top hats of the doormen on a really hectic Boat Race Night. That fountain just in front . . . the juxta-position of a top-hatted doorman and a fountain suggests an obvious possibility to those who—never having been to Oxford or Cambridge—indulge in the more rowdy and peace-disturbing forms of " ragging."

There is no need for any dissertation concerning the prices here. You can be well assured that your food and entertainment will cost quite a lot before you are through. Being forewarned thus, you know what to expect. Yet, unlike certain other well-known expensive places we know of, the prices at the Dorchester are justified. Completely and up to the hilt.

To delight your ears there is Moschetto's Orchestra ; yes, that self-same Moschetto you hear " on the air." And to dance to, there is Ambrose's Blue Lyres. What a band ! Lally, the leader, infuses the band with a rhythm only excelled by the better American bands. One can say nothing higher than that by way of praise. Would to Heaven we could have more of them and more often on the radio ; instead of so-and-so's dead-and-alive band, and what-d'you-call-'em's Funeral Sobstuff Moaners.

The Blue Lyres is—or should one say " are " ?—the cause of my enthusiasm for the Dorchester. A band that does not blast you off the dance floor, yet plays with zest, pep and genuine rhythm is, for most people, good cause enough for any prices to be charged. But then I'm somewhat of a fanatic where dance music is concerned—maybe because I've listened to it in eight capital cities of the world. Especially have I become a " fan " of the Blue Lyres, since they broadcast for eighty-five minutes only each week. The best band in England . . . less than an hour and a half.

Now then after that gratuitous effusion about the dance band—or rather, having heaved an unsolicited bouquet to the unheeding Blue Lyres, could there be higher praise than to say that the food is on the same plane as the dance band?

As it's Monday night I'm going to give you two

recipes from the chef and specimen menus of two
" nice little dinners"—choose the first dinner—and then
leave you to it. What time I switch on the radio and
tune in . . . quite right : the Blue Lyres.

Médaillon de Volaille Bûcheronne.

Composition. Have a good size fowl of about 3 lb.
weight, clean it and empty the same. Take 2
supremes from the wings, season with pepper from
the mill and salt. Plunge them into flour, after
this into melted butter and finally into bread-
crumbs.

Preparation. Put the supremes into a sauté pan,
and let cook on slow fire, put on the upper part of
them a farce of goose liver (foie gras), put on round
dish and at the last minute sprinkle over some finely
chopped parsley, fresh mushrooms and bread-crumbs,
a little fine chicken juice and a nice melted butter
noiselle.

The cooking must be quick at the last minute,
dish dressed rapidly and served burning hot. This
is essential.

Ciernikis (Hors-d'œuvre Russe).

Composition.

Take 4 oz. of white cheese

     4 oz. of flour

     4 oz. of butter

     3 eggs.

Mix all this together for a few moments, press the composition through a tammy cloth and add another 6 oz. of flour.

Preparation. With the mixture so obtained make small galettes (with a mould) of about $2\frac{1}{2}$ inches diameter and $\frac{1}{2}$ inch thick. Put them into boiling water for 15 to 18 minutes.

Take out at the moment, put in very hot Timbale and serve with melted butter poured over.

Cantaloup Frappé.
Caviar de Sterlet.

———

Consommé double Victoria.
Crème Rossolnick.

———

Délices de Sole Impérial.
Bouchées de Homard.

———

Mignonnette d'agneau de Printemps Francillon.
Pomme Annette.
Haricots verts fins à l'Anglaise.

———

Coq de Surrey en Cage.
Salade Diplomate.

———

Asperges de Lauris Wilhelmine.

———

Pêche glacée Carmen.
Friandises.

———

Canapés Pompadour.

Royal natives.

———

Vraie Tortue en Tasse.

———

Saumon d'Ecosse étuvé Chambord.
Cassolette de Concombres.

———

Côte de Caille Dodue Brillat Savarin.
Pointes d'Asperges à la Crème.

———

Selle de Pauillac Rôtie au Feu de Bois.
Pommes Mireille.
Petits pois nouveaux de Jersey.

———

Délices de volaille Talleyrand.
Salade Alice.

———

Cœur Flottant Tout Paris.
Corbeille de Douceurs.

———

Fruits.

There now! Big Ben has struck his wretched midnight and there's no more radio in this country.

Here's a little point from the wine list. There are forty-nine champagnes and only six liqueurs. Doesn't that tell you something? It should. They are such ordinary liqueurs too. Benedictine, Chartreuse, Cointreau, Crème de Menthe (ever tried burning off the fumes first?), Grand Marnier and Kummel.

Still, you can't have everything, I suppose.

WHEN IT'S TEA-TIME.

Tea-drinking in any country other than these our British Isles is nothing less than an ordeal. So far as the tea-growing countries are concerned, I speak without knowledge.

In countries north-west of the Balkans, however, tea-drinking is no fun. Russia produced the samovar ; if you like tea that way—then all right. As for tea in the Americas, why, it's out of the question.

This country of low incomes and high taxes is the only one to be considered, so far as tea-drinking is concerned. That's why various Chancellors of the Exchequer clap extra duties on tea whenever they can ; it's a sure fire winner, because the English have the tea habit so thoroughly.

Southern Europe sips its thimblesful of coffee-cum-chicory extract ; the Central Europeans swig their chocolate ; those citizens who inhabit the land west of a certain famous Statue of Liberty drink almost as much coffee per annum as they do bootleg booze.

The South Americans are weaned on coffee.

The English may toy with coffee and chocolate, but tea is the one hot non-alcoholic drink that matters in these rain-sodden islands over which waves the Union Jack : brave symbol of our rain-sodden hopes.

Walk along the streets of London, and judge for yourself whether or no we enjoy a cup of tea.

The Americans are prone to poke fun at the four o'clock tea-drinking in English offices ; but I've noticed they always accept a cup, if offered, should they happen to be in the office at that time ; and they are generally.

Personally, I find that office cup of tea to be of inestimable value. It revives flagging energies that have been dissipated by the enormous strain of working solidly from half-past two until four o'clock ; it stimulates the mind and spurs one on to make a final effort so that at five minutes to five as one puts down an empty cup, one has garnered strength enough to seize hat and stick and leave the office—exhausted but triumphant.

(A cumbersome sentence. . . .)

Even at mid-morning, about eleven o'clock that is, hundreds upon thousands of cups of tea are drunk by England's workers.

On English breakfast tables the teapot rules supreme.

It is between the hours of four and five in the afternoon that the whole country drinks tea ; wallows, paddles, splashes and swims in tea. Stocks may dive to hell, yet the broker will not forgo his cup of tea. An instantaneous decision may be required of the Cabinet : nothing doing—if it's tea-time.

So it goes without any further discourse on my part, that there are places aplenty in London town where cups of tea may be had. Any amount of tea-shops ; cafés ;

restaurants ; pâtisseries and the like. Some very elegant ; some not so swell ; plenty of tea-shops of many kinds that are just ordinary ; and vast numbers of resorts that are just places where you can get tea.

You can imbibe it from fragile porcelain cups to the sweet strains of Debussy—as at the Carlton, Claridge's and the like ; or you can gulp it from thick China mugs to the sozzling noises made by taxi drivers and other patrons of that ilk. No matter where you go, it's still tea, and still the nation's beverage.

Neither of the milieus quoted appeals to me much ; from a tea-drinking point of view that is.

Moderation and " the happy medium " in all things, is a perfectly good maxim to observe.

Now, there's *Gunter's* at 72, *New Bond Street*. In many little ways not nearly so nice as the place they had on the other side of the street. Gilt chairs ; wonderful cakes which you choose for yourself from a tremendous display ; the best ice-cream in London. The patrons of Gunter's are people shopping in the neighbourhood ; uncles and aunts with nieces and nephews.

Nor must I forget that Gunter's have a shop in Berkeley Square ; you know ; where " strange, terrible, lovely things happen." I think this shop has a mid-Victorian air about it. Too many aspidistra-type of plants scattered around.

Gunter's make beautiful cakes for weddings, christenings, birthdays and other such functions and anniversaries as have to be remembered by a display of white icing. These cakes are not cheap, as I know only too well, but they are the best in the world.

Almost next door to Gunter's in Bond Street, is *Barbellion* at 70, *New Bond Street*. This place is smaller and somewhat more Frenchified. Go upstairs and get a table near to the window. It's amusing to watch the crowd.

Then, of course, there's *Rumpelmayer* at 72, *St. James's Street, S.W.1*. This place is represented on the Riviera ; in Paris and also in New York. The Hotel St. Moritz facing Central Park spreads a benevolent roof over Rumpelmayer in New York.

More gilt chairs ; a music-dispensing trio of piano, violin and violoncello help to muffle the sounds of gâteau-mastication. It is pleasant to drop into this tea-room for " the cup that cheers but does not inebriate " after an exhausting afternoon " ridin' herd " over a group of tourist Americans who have spent their time laying bets as to which is the Prince of Wales's bedroom window in St. James's Palace close by.

Stewart's is at the Marble Arch ; in Regent Street, and also on the corner of Old Bond Street and Piccadilly. This is a restaurant with waitresses. At eleven o'clock in the morning it is much patronized by women carrying rustling paper packages ; women who feel a need for a fortifying snack of Bath buns with butter and cups of tea or coffee. Stewart's have also excellent ice-cream sodas of all kinds.

Throughout London there are many branches of *Fuller's*. Fuller's Walnut Cake is a good thing to know ; that is, if you like walnuts.

Ridgeway's have a tea-shop in Piccadilly. Suggest you try their blend called " Her Majesty's Blend."

Kardomah is the Oriental name given to another tea-shop and café with depots in Piccadilly and Fleet Street. They think quite a lot of their beverages here : and rightly, too.

The Aerated Bread Company, more generally known as " The A.B.C.," and the *Express Dairy Company* have chains of cheap-type tea-shops. Catering to the masses. Also *W. Hill* and " *J.P.*" tea-shops are to be met with here and there. I've seen these places from the outside only, so you can have all the thrill of exploring the inside of them.

Buszard's in Oxford Street have a long-established reputation for the making of wedding-cakes. Having had no call to order such a confection within recent times, I'm not *au fait* with Buszard's. Anyway, the place has been taken over by the A.B.C., although still retaining the old name.

Westminster Cafés and *Mecca Cafés* have places scattered around London. Especially in office districts ; catering to thirsty typists, I suppose.

Then we must not omit our old friend *Slater's* with its female orchestras. . . .

*   *   *   *   *

So much then for a scampering survey of London's general tea-catering arrangements. Because I don't happen to have mentioned the establishments of J. Lyons & Co., Ltd. in this section, is due to my belief that you would take them for granted. The original Lyons tea-shop, being in Piccadilly, is quite near Ridgeway's place. So you can look reverently at the one and then drink tea thankfully in the other.

There is in London an amazing swarm of tea-shops located in basements, sub-basements, semi-basements, attics, such as Joan's Kitchen, Sally's Pantry, Busy Bees, Gracious Ladies, Cubby Hole, Happy Gnomes, the Inglenook. Know the places I mean? They are operated invariably by gentlewomen; and generally in reduced circumstances at that.

Now, I have nothing against " gentlewomen in reduced circumstances " running tea-shops. In fact, am all for it. Keeps them out of mischief; gives them something to do; something to do that may be profitable financially—and would be profitable if these same gentlewomen would not be above taking hints from the ordinary tea-shops.

Especially if they learnt first to give genuinely good food that was value for money; secondly, proper ser-vice; thirdly, to cut out that foolish haughtiness they show to mere customers. It's that attitude of "I've-seen-better-days-and-it's-a-hell-of-an-honour-for-you-to-have-me-bring-you-this-beastly-tea-for-which-we-charge-outrageous-prices" that annoys me and hundreds of other potentially good customers who would welcome a tea-room not inundated with *hoi polloi*. Welcome it, I say, provided the surroundings were pleasant, and the food decent and reasonably priced.

When such a tea-room is to be found—and if you have patience it can be found—then you may thank your stars and patronize it joyfully. The majority of tea-room hunters are not so fortunate as to find a good one, and are thus compelled to go either to a bad one or to one of Lyons' well-deserving but somewhat noisy emporia.

The above condemnation may seem too general and too sweeping; it is not intended to be. It is because the few good exceptions are so excellent that they only serve to throw the others into a still less favourable light.

There is a place in Wardour Street between Gerrard Street and Shaftesbury Avenue—called *Mrs. Brown's Little Tea-shop. Lunches Too, Ltd.* It is worthy of particularly pleasant comment on my part for two reasons. First of all, the name : the " Lunches Too " part is a good notion. Secondly, the food and service approximate most nearly to the public's demand of such in tea-shops. Anyway, this place is generally known as Mrs. Brown's. Which is perfectly sensible.

Some years ago a worthy gentleman by the name of

Billy Brasher started a small restaurant-tea-shop-lounge with the name of the *Stage Door*. The keynote of the clientèle being theatrical. So successful was this venture that Brasher started the *Prompt Corner* in Rupert Street. Now the Stage Door has folded up though the Prompt Corner is still going strong. Here will be gathered the junior members of the theatres and film studios ; those lesser luminaries who lie like flat fish to bolster up their own courage in the hopes of better times to come.

Down in South Kensington, not so many stones' throw from the Natural History Museum is the *Russian Tea-Rooms*. That should tell you plenty. In St. Martin's Lane is the *Samovar*—Caucasian is the keynote of this place. Whilst in the Fulham Road, near the Queen's Elm, is the *Casserole*—the nationality being Russian : the motif, red lacquer.

Alas ! That the world's very best tea-room is no more. I refer to the Empire Tea-Room of the Trocadero.

Chelsea is a fruitful field for tea-rooms. Earlier in this book there was mention made at length of one of them. In addition, there is the *Lombard* also in Cheyne Walk at the corner of Church Street.

When all's said and done the best tea from the flavour point of view is that sold by Lyons. No matter what anyone may say to the contrary. Whether you choose Indian or China blend, the best procurable is

to be found in the teapots of these tea-shops. With
no exceptions.

HUNGARIA RESTAURANT, 14, *Regent Street, S.W.1.*

What a cigar-technique ! With what an air does the
Signor Joseph Vecchi offer the bale of cigars to a
purchaser of that sometimes-not-too-frequent weed of
Havana.

Such was my first impression upon revisiting Hungaria Restaurant after a lapse of two years. We were
luncheoning in the restaurant proper : I say " we,"
for it was " we " and not " I " ! And so it was that
we were enabled to watch the cigar-technique mentioned. On a plate was a bale or bundle of cigars
whose composite waist was girt with a yellow ribbon :
carefully, Signor Vecchi picked up the bale with both
hands and held it so that the rounded ends of the
cigars were displayed to the purchaser. The latter
made his choice—from somewhere in the centre of the
bale, and Signor Vecchi pushed out the chosen cigar
with a gentle pressure of his two thumbs—and there
you are ! Absolutely no deception and nothing up his
sleeve ! We wondered whether Signor Vecchi does his
little trick only in the case of expensive cigars.

Hungaria Restaurant is, I believe, the advertising
medium of Hungary for its wines. For corroboration
of that statement see the wine list, which is the most
attractive of its kind to be found in London. The

joint managers are Mr. Joseph Vecchi and Mr. Joseph Benini—names that seem ultra-Italian. Anyway, Mr. Vecchi makes no bones about it—he comes from Bologna and is proud of the fact. Mr. Benini lurks, who knows where?

The food is Hungarian right enough. The decorations of the place, also. Inasmuch as the crests of Hungarian towns are placed on the walls. The music is Hungarian: Rigo and his famous Gipsy Band. They all look uncommonly civilized; not at all like the gipsies one sees on Epsom Downs. Nevertheless, there is the full complement of violins, xylophones and much pizzicato and "noisy-cats" playing; and of course, that "oh so sahd, sahd" gipsy music that is dragged slowly and reluctantly from gipsy instruments by gipsy fingers, what time gipsy hearts are overflowing with gipsy-speculations. This band plays unusually well, and marks good rhythm for dancing.

By the way, make a note on your engagement pad that Tuesday is the best night to frivol at the Hungaria —for the good and sufficient reason that there is an extension of drinking licence until 2 a.m. An important point: D.O.R.A. permits you to get squiffed more leisurely.

Let's talk of the wines. Hungaria is proud of them. They come from the Royal Hungarian State Wine Cellars—and are not a penny the more expensive on the score of that boop-a-doop announcement. To read the

148

wine list is in itself a thing of joy. For each wine is named in Hungarian and its nearest equivalent in more Occidental languages :—French or English,—and after that comes a detailed description of the wine, so it's entirely your own fault if you order something that you don't like after trying it. Bear in mind that Hungary breeds fleet horses and strong wines. I know ; believe me I know, to my cost ! For, drinking a bottle of Number 5—which is " a very fine white muscatel wine, medium dry . . ." the balance of the day was spent in sleeping. That's what Number 5 does, if you drink it at lunch-time. But it is, without doubt, a delightful wine, and most reasonable in price, being eight shillings. A couple of dollars, that is.

If you like red wine, try Number 13. " Bull's blood," so it is termed colloquially. This is called " a dry strong wine "—and requires a strong head and constitution to withstand its insidious effects.

There are twenty-seven other Hungarian wines from which to make your choice ; prices ranging from six shillings a bottle to £3 5s. the half-bottle in the case of Number 25. A Tokay wine of 1889, which is very rare. Too rare for most people to pay that price for it.

Hungaria Restaurant is to be congratulated on having a choice of thirty-five different liqueurs. Also seven special Hungarian ones. Try the Hungarian Apricot Brandy. What a liqueur ! To have another savours of sacrilege almost.

Should you feel very expansive and very expensive you can now buy a bottle of authentic 1830 Cognac. There are a few bottles of it left. The price? A mere bagatelle : to rich people who collect rarities. A paltry £21 (105 dollars) per bottle. Not even a New York bootlegger would have the courage to charge that price.

Undoubtedly, Hungaria is a restaurant where you can have a thoroughly good time browsing through the wine list ; you know—browsing and sampling. Many a long day could one spend thus, given the chance.

With regard to food. There are but few who do not like Hungarian cooking once they have tried it ; perhaps because it is represented so often by paprika sauces—which are pretty to look at in addition to being excellent to taste.

If you like, you can get a four-course luncheon at five shillings and sixpence. You can, and it is excellent ; but if you are wise you'll choose from one of the following recipes which I have tried, eaten, enjoyed and hereby solemnly pronounce to be deserving of your closest attention. First of all, we will give you the Hungarian names :

Turbot-Magyarosan.
Paprikás-cabillaud.
Almàs-retes.

Let's take them in the order named.
The Turbot-Magyarosan which is :

Hungarian Turbot (at three shillings and sixpence per
portion).

Three onions chopped fine ; 2 oz. lard ; 2 lb.
turbot ; 1 lb. new potatoes ; 1 tablespoonful paprika powder ; salt ; 4 tomatoes.

Melt the lard in a saucepan, add the chopped
onions and allow to fry only a few minutes without
browning. Then add the paprika powder and stir
well. Add quickly one pint of water and simmer for
ten minutes. Cut the fish in eight pieces, salt it,
then dip fish in flour and place it in simmering
sauce. Then add potatoes cut in half, with quar-
tered tomatoes, and pinch of salt. Cover, and place
saucepan in the oven and cook fish for fifteen minutes.
When serving place potatoes round the fish.

A good and satisfying dish ; there's a Friday every
week !
The next, translated, is :

Paprika Chicken (three shillings a time).

One chicken, medium size ; 2 oz. lard ; 2 onions ;
1 teaspoonful of paprika powder ; 1 teacup of cream ;
1 pinch of salt.

Cut the chicken into pieces, melt the lard in a
saucepan and allow to fry until yellow. Stir in

paprika powder, add chicken and half a cup of water, cover and stew until tender. Add cream and boil for three minutes.

Serve chicken with own gravy, and small flour dumplings or rice.

These are the dishes with the p-pretty, p-pink, p-paprika p-sauce.

Now we come to Almàs-Retes, which in German is *Apfelctrudel*; and the nearest English equivalent is Baked Apple Roll : a brutal, non-committal name which does not begin to describe the thing.

Read this recipe and judge for yourself.

Almàs-Retes.

One lb. of flour ; 1 oz. of butter ; 1 egg ; 1 tablespoonful of white vinegar ; 1 pinch of salt ; $\frac{1}{2}$ pint of warm water ; 3 lb. sliced apples ; 2 oz. sultanas ; 2 oz. of sliced almonds ; 2 oz. of castor-sugar ; 1 pinch cinnamon.

Mix the flour, butter, egg, salt and vinegar with warm water, and allow to stand for $\frac{3}{4}$ hour. While the paste is standing, cover table with a table-cloth and sprinkle flour all over. When the paste has stood for the required time, place in the middle of the covered table.

(*The next operation is extremely delicate and upon its proper execution depends ultimate success.*)

Take the paste with both hands, and gently pull

until it becomes thinned out. Allow to dry for a few minutes. Brush with a little melted butter, and cover completely with the sliced apples, raisins, sliced almonds and cinnamon. Take the cloth containing the roll and roll together. Remove the cloth and place the roll on a baking-tray, brush with a little melted butter, and cook for 20 minutes in a moderate oven.

Would you like to do all that on your gas range at home, or will you take the more logical step and pay a mere measly shilling for a huge portion of it at Hungaria ? The cautionary note in the middle of that recipe is most delightful.

If you are fond of mushroom soup, and you should be for it is a worthy dish, there's none better in London than the special mushroom soup that can be made to order here.

There's one thing I want to know, and I was too shy to ask either Mr. Vecchi, or Mr. Rigo—orchestra leader. In the contract for the orchestra, is there a clause stipulating that there will be so many " Hungarian shouts " per session of playing ? Or does each musician get a bonus according to the number of " Hungarian shouts " he interpolates ?

As an appetizer try a slice of Mortadella. It is a sausage, ten inches in diameter. It comes from Bologna ; and so does Mr. Vecchi.

DANCE RESTAURANTS

It is a great pity to have to record it, but there is an appalling sameness in the menus of smart dine-sup-and-dance places. The differences in such restaurants are to be found in the decorations, the band and the entertainment. Certainly not in the clientèle ; for if you move from one dance place to another, you will soon discover that everyone has done that same thing. There is about the food a uniform standard of quality which palls on one. So, in one short chapter, we will dispose of the more elegant resorts of the élite.

Have you got a radio—or wireless set, if you call it that ? Then the name Roy Fox is not unknown to you. He was at the *Monseigneur* in Piccadilly—but you knew that, too. Douglas Byng, who entertains there, is very amusing.

By the way, here's a little tip which may prove helpful to you. In contemplation of an evening at Monseigneur, make your arrangements beforehand ; agree on food, drink and prices. You'll find the *maître d'hôtel* not only agreeable but helpful ; and if you are not overburdened with this world's wealth, state the fact to him clearly ; put him " on his mettle " to do the best he can for you within your price limitations. You'll not be disappointed.

Then there is *Malmaison* in *Stratton Street, Mayfair*. Please be so good as to accent the last word of that address. Mr. Sovrani, who had the Sovrani Grill in Jermyn Street, now dispenses highly-priced food and excellent entertainment to three grades of people. One: those who can afford to ignore the depression. Two: those who want to make a splash. Three: those who can get themselves attached to either of the first two groups.

Malmaison is so popular that taxi-cabs have to be arranged in tiers ; one top of another, whilst private cars are parked in the grill rooms of less-successful neighbouring restaurants.

Kit Cat at the top of the *Haymarket*. This is one of the Old Guard of dancing and supping places. Although the trend is to patronize those west of Piccadilly Circus, there is still an ever-faithful band of devotees to whom the Kit Cat caters with all of its old time *joie de vivre*.

Café de Paris in *Coventry Street* is next to the Rialto Cinema. It occupies the premises of what used to be the Elysée Restaurant.

Under the same management is the *Café Anglais* in *Leicester Square*—once called the Cavour, a much nicer name. I like the cocktail bar here : it's such a little, pip-squeak affair. Both these supper-dance places are expensive. There's no question but that they dispense food and entertainment of the highest possible standard. Roy Fox's band is here, now.

Kettner's in *Church Street*, *Soho*, has " gone gay " in

recent years. No longer is it good and quiet ; now it is good and noisy. Women lunch in swarms at Kettner's. You can dine and dance here. Not like it was in the " good old days ; " when the management relied solely on good food and excellent cooking for keeping its clientèle. Not that the cuisine is diminished in any way, mark you ; it's not. Only, by being modern enough to have music Kettner's has lost a little of its distinctive cachet and, incidentally, the high esteem with which some of the older generation were wont to regard it. That will not affect Kettner's to any great extent, to be sure. This restaurant was quick to realize the modern demand for entertainment and acted accordingly.

You can still get specially-chosen special specialities each day : such dishes as bouillabaisse, veau à la Strogonoff, ravioli and so on. Reminders that serve to maintain the illusion that Kettner's is as it has been always.

I feel it in my bones that in a few years' time the *Waldorf* in *Aldwych* is going to be known as " that funny old hotel 'way down in the City." So rapid has been the Westward trend of life that the Waldorf has been left stranded. It is a pleasant-enough caravanserai. Nothing special about it : Frenchified cooking that is eminently satisfactory. 'Twas here, many years ago, that Joseph Conrad brought me for a celebration luncheon, and introduced to my notice those piscatorial midgets known as whitebait. It took me hours to eat them—taking off heads and tails.

You can dance at the Waldorf.

The Carlton Grill Room in the *Haymarket* is one of those eminently excellent places to which business men take " prospects " for lunch ; padres do themselves well here ; and those people who want to be assured that they will be looked after well and truly.

The *maître d'hôtel* is a sympathetic kindly soul who has a weakness for two different kinds of customer. The one who orders confidently and well : the other who does not know what to order, admits it frankly and appeals to M. Charles for help and guidance. It is an excellent place also to go on your own, or to take an important friend of the gentler sex ; by which is meant an " important friend " who is a connoisseur of good food.

Here is a small point that should engage the notice of all cheese-lovers. At the Carlton, Camembert and Brie are always in perfect condition ; just exactly right. There are times when nothing " hits the spot " so truly as a morsel of ripe Brie. You must not neglect the Carlton. Why, the name has become a synonym for excellence. " Excellence " is considered good enough for the majority of people.

* * * * *

Now let me guide you gently up the Haymarket again and along Piccadilly to one of my more favourite places. Hatchett's to wit. Or to give the place its full name, rank and number,

HATCHETT'S WHITE HORSE CELLARS,
67a, Piccadilly, W.1.

This place has a deceptive appearance, for the entrance is inconspicuous, meagre, stingy almost. Be not dismayed. For what Hatchett's lacks in window frontage on Piccadilly it makes up by going downwards, and then spreading itself so that there is another egress in Dover Street.

Also in Dover Street is located Hatchett's American Bar and Quick Lunch Counter presided over by the genial Sam. How long Sam has been with this place I cannot say ; anyhow, he knows me well enough by now to reach for the Canadian Club whisky as soon as I poke my nose within his domains ; and, off and on, I've been doing that over a number of years.

There's another bar at the Piccadilly side of Hatchett's. This is presided over by Mesdames Jeanne and Scottie, who are known throughout the length and breadth of the British Empire. This bar is a rendezvous for returned exiles, Empire builders and other adventuring Britons : who inscribe their name and outpost-address within a book kept specially for that purpose. The idea being that others can read and thus learn if neighbourhood friends—or enemies— are back in Deah Old Lundun.

Downstairs is another Cocktail Lounge. A delightful place to have " the other half " whilst waiting for the invariably late girl friend. The later she is, the more " other halves " you can drink, until you don't care if she never turns up at all. It is comfortable ; the service is quick and quiet ; the drinks are all that they should be. What more can a man ask for, other than cash and a thirst ? The restaurant leads out of this and is a charming room divided into nooks and hideaways, so that every table is a corner table. A clever little trick, that table arrangement.

The first thing to impress you is the atmosphere. This restaurant is well below the street level ; yet 'tis cool in summer—by which I infer those occasional hot days—and warm in winter ; the air is clear and fresh with no smoke or smells of cooking. So I asked Mr. Rolph, the cheery manager, how such a pleasant atmosphere was achieved. He did explain it to me— twice, and very carefully. Every four minutes, the air is taken out ; examined for defective parts ; washed, brushed and combed ; parted neatly in the middle, and . . . maybe I have forgotten what exactly is done to it, only, whatever it is, is done every four minutes.

Mr. Rolph has two characteristics. One is smoking cigarettes through especially-short cigarette holders. The other is, tapping heartily on the floor of the bar when the pressure is insufficient for the beer engine. The tapping has an immediate effect on George, who is somewhere in the nether regions, and whose job it is to maintain correct pressures. Mr. Rolph has a habit of being everywhere and supervising everything. There's nobody more competent, either ; and the staff knows it ! That's why there is such perfect service at Hatchett's ; the boss is very much on the job all the time.

Hatchett's like you to be frank with them if you cannot afford to spend much money. They like to save you money, on the theory that you will come more often. Also, it is a genuine pleasure to M. Joseph to see smiles of delighted contentment on the faces of satisfied customers. Go to M. Joseph—he is *maître d'hôtel*, by the way—and say, " I'm inviting two ladies and a gentleman for dinner to-night, and can only afford a total of so much. What do you suggest ? "

M. Joseph will produce paper and pencil and after some rapid figuring announce, " Certainly, sir ! I will give you a most excellent dinner of so-and-so and so-and-so and what d'ye-call-'em ; a bottle of such-and-such with a half-bottle of something else for the ladies ; coffee for all ; cigars for you two gentlemen ; and liqueurs."

There you are ! No fuss or bother. The dinner will be well-balanced—excellently blended with the wines —perfectly cooked and served. Nor will you have to make surreptitious search for that emergency money supply tucked into some inaccessible pocket !

Special Business Lunch at two shillings and sixpence is another feature of this place. Here are two specimen menus.

Roast Sirloin of Beef.
Escalope de Veau Viennoise.
Celery Braisé.
Pommes Sauté.

———

Crème Caramel
or
Fromage.

Roast Veal and Bacon.
Bitock à la russe.
Spinach.
Mashed Potatoes.

———

Glace Panachée
or
Fromage.

These strike me as being remarkably good value for money in a place having the cachet of Hatchett's. With them, you can drink as you wish ; tankards of draught lager or beer seem to be popular with everyone. So, if you become an habitué of Hatchett's you can cut down your expensive habits and cultivate a liking for beer.

Jot these items in your notebook.

Four-course luncheon at four shillings.

Theatre dinners at 6s. 6d. and at 7s. 6d., of five and

six courses respectively. These dinners are served as
from six o'clock. A few minutes earlier, and it would
have been " high tea ! "

Draught lager is ninepence or one and threepence.

Wine by the glass at a shilling a time, or in large
carafes for four shillings and small carafes for two
shillings.

Here are Hatchett's specialities, the memories of
which cause the aforementioned Empire builders to
gulp heavily behind their matted, unkempt beards.

	s.	d.
Pamplemousse Hatchett's.	2	0
Marmite Excelsior .	2	6
Sole Alice	4	0
Filet de Bœuf Grillé Eros	4	6
Pêche ou Poire Hatchett's	3	6
Banane Glacée Juliette	3	0
Crêpes Suzette	3	0
Soufflé Parisien	3	6

The only one I don't know is the first. Pample-
mousse sounds like a name given to his lady friend by
an infatuated German banker.

My attempts to wheedle the recipes for any of the
above met with cold, blank, chilly disapproval. With
silence. From which I deduced that such recipes were
not for publication. However, smiles were the order

of the day when I suggested meekly that recipes of other specialities would be of interest.

After due cogitation it was conceded that I might have two recipes on the condition that I sat down then and there and tried them out.

Here they are :

Lobster Delmonico.

Take a nice-cooked lobster, slice it and warm it up in butter. Prepare a rich cream sauce, beat up in same the yolks of eggs, mix with salt, cayenne, sherry, and add a little brandy. Then make a border of Duchesse potatoes, arrange the sliced lobster artistically in the dish, pour the sauce over and glace under a salamander. Just before serving sprinkle over the dish chopped hard-boiled egg, parsley, chopped truffles and coral.

Poularde Maison Hatchett's.

Cook a nice white poularde in butter. Pour in saucepan some white wine and add chopped fresh tomatoes. Decorate dish with bouchée of mushrooms à la crème, arrange fond artichoke set with points of asparagus and a slice of truffle and potatoes Parisienne. Put momentarily into oven and serve.

Hatchett's White Horse Cellars has—or have—been flourishing since the days of coaching. In fact, it was founded in the year 1720. A date which eluded me, until I was reminded that that was the year of the fateful South Sea Bubble—forerunner of our present-day stock market crashes.

SELFRIDGE'S, *Oxford Street, W.1.*

"*The Hanging Gardens of London.*"

" It is interesting to note that 1,500 tons of soil, earth, rocks, etc., were used in the construction of these gardens, and each autumn 30,000 bulbs are planted, converting them in the spring and summer to one of the prettiest spots in London. They are the only gardens of their kind in the world."

The above is a quotation. Thereby hangs a tale. There are occasions when I want to buy something that can only be bought at the right price *chez* Selfridge. So I go shopping in that store. So do at least eighty-five millions of other people ; chiefly women. They all express a simultaneous desire to patronize the counter from which I make a humble purchase—maybe cheap socks ; maybe not.

The resultant chaos and confusion is both unnerving and exhausting. So a shopping expedition at this store means a visit for recuperative purposes to the roof garden. Oh ! Now we are getting to the object of the quotation.

Slinking unobtrusively into a lift—you call them " elevators " in New York—I murmur " Roof Garden " and close my eyes—nearly. Just keeping them open enough to play that fascinating game of Button Counting; the buttons being on the gaitered legs of the cute lift girls who announce: " Furst Flo-ah! Laydees' Wa-ah; lang-jeree; reddee-may-eed coschooms: go-ing up-p-p!" And so on until she carols blithely " Roo-of Gahden. Top!" And there I am.

Here, then, can you find a pleasant sanctuary from frenzied women shoppers downstairs—each of whom forgets what she really came to buy and goes home with masses of useless things which she displays triumphantly—" such bargains, my dear!"

The Roof Garden has improved out of all recognition during the last few years. It changes its appearance, for the better, almost overnight. So that it is no small pleasure to sit in some nook among the flowers and quaff an ice-cream soda, which by the way you can damned well get for yourself from the counter in exchange for a ticket to the value of your purchase. This ticket is got from a desk. This rigmarole is not so involved as it sounds, and it dispenses with a top-heavy staff.

Having got your ice-cream soda, parfait, sundae, frappé or Banana Royal, you carry off the spoils in search of a secluded how-d'ye-do in which to enjoy it. All the best nooks will be taken; so scowl at the occupier and grab a second-best nook; " 'midst the wafting fragrance of countless flowers." That also is a quotation. As a matter of mathematical interest, surely " countless " is used inaccurately in this case : thirty thousand bulbs are planted, each one producing a certain number of blooms—the total should not be countless, by any manner of means.

Selfridge's has a right to boost the Roof Garden ; there is no more pleasant a place on a hot summer's day, which is centrally located and such a boon to *hoi polloi*.

My casual request for a menu to keep ; the explanations that followed and the general pother resulting, sent the Publicity Department of Selfridge's on my trail, like a pack of bloodhounds. I wanted a menu, so as to verify my writings ? Certainly ! Have a lot ; take two ! All manner of menus were thrust upon me. Big ones ; little ones ; gaudy ones ; monthly shopping guides ; weekly shopping guides, and the Lord knows what other literature besides. I was snowed under with information. All done so pleasantly and with such smiles ; and that word " smiles " forms the clue to the success of Selfridge's store. You are served expeditiously throughout the whole building—always with cheerful, pleasant smiles.

It wasn't until I had chartered a taxi to carry me and my gratuitously-donated literature home, that I discovered a *bonne bouche* had been thrust into my pocket. Entitled " 101 Unusual Services ! Do you know,

Selfridge's——" then follow the services : everything from wart-removing and cleaning pipes to taking the pain from aching feet.

Completely bewildered by all this, I turned over the page and saw the quotations I have given you—in an illustrated description of the Roof Garden.

The description is too poetical ; too romantic. Not a word in the whole thing about the ice-cream sodas and so on—which, by the way, are every bit as good as those sold by Sherry's in New York. The description tells you plenty about " goldfish in fringed ponds ; " " tranquil atmosphere of an old-world garden ; " and " trim green lawns." There's nothing about Chocolate Malted Milk Shake, 9d. Or Egg-Flip—Our Style, 9d.

Now, in addition to the Roof Garden there is a Soda Fountain in the north-east corner of the Ground Floor. It's busy all the time ; proof that Selfridge's know their soda-fountain business.

Also there is a straightforward restaurant-cum-tea-room on the top floor. If you are agreeable, sweet ladies of Omaha, Nebraska and other God-forsaken parts of the United States, we will take you along to this restaurant and give you the surprise of your young, middle-aged and elderly lives. Real honest-to-good-ness American dishes, cooked American style ; and we don't mean maybe. If you look at the following items it will make your home towns seem just around

the corner; it will do much to assuage those yearnings
for Little Neck, and Bear Creek that beset you when
visiting Europe.

		s.	d.	
1.	American Creamed Lentil, Frizzled Bacon and Devilled Tomato . .	1	6	or (approx. 36c. at par)
2.	Boston Baked Beans .	0	6	,, 12c. ,,
3.	Cottage Cheese (Home Made) . . .	0	9	,, 18c. ,,
4.	Stewed Sweet Corn .	0	6	,, 12c. ,,
5.	Hot Waffle, butter and Maple Syrup . .	1	0	,, 24c. ,,
6.	Corned Beef Hash and Poached Egg . .	2	3	,, 54c. ,,
7.	American Pancakes with Maple Syrup and butter	1	0	,, 24c. ,,
8.	Oyster Stew. . .	3	0	,, 72c. ,,
9.	Chicken à la King .	2	9	,, 66c. ,,
10.	Coco-nut Cream Pie .	0	9	,, 18c. ,,

There are plenty of other American dishes from
which to make your choice: plenty. There are
carpers who might say to you, " Why the something-
or-other do you come to Europe, and then eat American
dishes ? " Yet, it is understandable ; that craving for
an occasional meal that smacks of the safe, sane and
familiar. Having much in sympathy with such nos-

talgia is the primary reason for the detailed mention of these American dishes at Selfridge's ; that, and that they are the genuine dyed-in-the-wool things ; and excellently cooked and served withal.

If you have patronized the Diners in New York or other cities, you will recollect the slap, dash, yell, bang that accompanies all orders. That is a bit of atmosphere you forgo when luncheoning à l'Américain in this store.

To whom do you owe a debt of thanks for this little sample of your United States ? To none other than the originator : Mr. Gordon Selfridge. It is a well-founded fact that the moulding of his business methods had origin in Chicago : Queen of the Middle West—or, as a New Yorker once called it, " a machine-gun arsenal surrounded by prairie." A libellous commentary on placid Chicago.

The next day having any pretensions to warmth will find scores of bargain-dazed shoppers in the Roof Garden ; bibbing Strawberry Ice-Cream Sodas with the aid of two straws and a spoon. Just guzzling and revelling. For these ice-cream sodas are . . . " swellegant ! "

DE HEM'S, *Macclesfield Street, Shaftesbury Avenue, W.*1.

Just a word or two about this place. It's a conglomerate oyster dive, snack bar, chop house and public-house.

Cold snacks, such as ham, veal pie, lobster salad and the like; oysters of the Whitstable and Dutch varieties; hot table d'hôte luncheon and dinners in dining-room upstairs; also, at the few tables by the snack counter; and then a large horse-shoe-shaped drinking bar. Downstairs, more oyster-gorging accommodation.

The whole place is as crowded and chaotic as the preceding paragraph. During the rush hours, which means drinking hours, De Hem's is a seething mass of customers.

There is no place in London where one can eat and drink so heartily in the British manner in such a hectic scrum. For around the bar will be serried ranks of topers blocking up the gangway and overflowing into the snack bar preserves; there will be those who steer erratic courses from drink to lobster salad and back again—though there is no need for them to do so as drinks are served at the snack bar. Waitresses carrying trays from the kitchen shove or push a way through the crowds. Barmaids cackle and joke with bibulous customers; futile talk, laughter and alcohol-engendered humour all help to make confusion worse confounded.

Noise, heat, stuffiness, fumes of food, drink, tobacco and humanity all blend to create an atmosphere thick enough to cut with a knife. Yet, what is so extraordinary, the patrons of De Hem's seem to be oblivious to the discomfort ; seem to like it, even. For there is no doubt but that this place has achieved a great and fairly solid popularity.

English fare, plain but good and well-cooked, is the order of the day here. Welsh Rarebits—at the ridiculously low price of only sixpence—sizzling hot, are a great speciality and I recommend them as worthy of your attention. With a large ice-cold lager drawn from the wood, this is luncheon enough. Of course, an you feel like it, have a dozen oysters before ; two dozen even.

The patrons are clearly of definite cliques. The clique that is most noticeable is composed of young men with slicked-backed hair and oil-stained trousers : two signs proclaiming them to be motor-car salesmen —the modern, unromantic counterpart of horse-copers. These young men drink beer from tankards ; not once or twice do they have these tankards refilled, but many, many times. Another very conspicuous clique is that of the betting fraternity. No mistaking them, with their hail-fellow-well-met attitude toward each other and the world in general.

There are so many good points about De Hem's that it would not come amiss to say that a small piece of ice in a drink is not so nice as a drink that is properly cooled before being served. Admittedly, there may be difficulties in achieving the latter, yet such difficulties are not insuperable.

RULE'S, *Maiden Lane, W.C.2.*

Now there are any number of other pubs and chop houses in London deserving mention for this reason or for that. Perhaps none more so than Rule's in Maiden Lane, at the back of the Adelphi and Vaudeville theatres. This place is under the control of genial Tom Bell, who plays golf. That statement concerning golf is not so inconsequential as it may appear to be. A goodly percentage of Rule's patrons is of the sporting fraternity. Horses, football and golf. Mr. Bell plays golf.

There are many points about this place. It is a great haunt of the literary and artistic groups ; provided the members thereof have money enough to pay their bills at Rule's. For, let it be said here and now, this restaurant is not one of the cheapest in London. Not by several long chalks.

Its chief claim to popular fame is the beauty of the barmaids. For them as likes barmaids, Rule's must be a paradise on earth. Blonde and brunette are represented, so the drinker at the bar can take his choice as to which one shall be the recipient of his confidences and lamentations.

Not so long ago, Rule's decided to dispense with barmaids and installed male bartenders. The venture was not a success. What, no barmaids ? Let's go somewhere else—said the drinkers. And they did.

So the barmaids were recalled, and all the " old gang " came trotting back.

Certainly these gentle creatures give a definite cachet to the place. Coarse language is non-existent ; the barmaids are adept at putting too-friendly customers in their places ; they always act as guards to the benefit of customers, inasmuch as they refuse to let them drink too much ; and generally, these barmaids are worth their weight in gold—which, in certain instances, is quite a lot.

Being close to theatre-land, Rule's has collected a large number of ancient programmes which are framed and hung on the walls. Sporting prints, cartoons and caricatures all help to fill up space. To many people such decorations are of interest ; and to such, I would call their attention to the truly excellent collection that is displayed on the walls at Rule's.

One sits on settees covered in red plush or " ploosh " as a waiter called it. That is, if you get a wall-side table, and you will be wise to do so if one is available. When ordering your food be firmer than the Rock of Gibraltar. There are waiters here who take it into their heads to bring you things other than your wish ; if you are weak, and accept what they bring, then more fool you. When you give your order, make the waiter repeat it to you item by item.

There is no doubt but that the cooking is excellent. It certainly should be, for the prices are at the lofty end of the scale for a chop house. Particularly do I advise something from the grill. A chump chop at Rule's is all that such a cutlet should be. A snack for a full-sized man ; none of your Frenchy chops reminiscent of the loins of a Pekinese.

Careful note should be made of the head waiter here. He is so supremely sure of himself : so positively the monarch of all he surveys.

There is a room upstairs to which it is advisable to resort if you are a mixed party. It is somewhat less noisy and less patronized by the more staunch supporters of the bar. Even then, you should get a table at the end of the room farthest away from the bar, should the enjoyment of your food in comparative peace be your aim. If absolute quiet is your objective then an English chop house of this calibre is the last place to choose. Beauteous barmaids act like candles to young and old alike : and they do make it a more cheerful business : this having a drink I mean.

It is many years since I was one of a group that dined with a certain regularity at this place. I remember with horror the unutterably dreary tone with which Gillespie would recite a few miles of poetry when he had " drink taken " as the Scots term it.

Subsequent visits in later years have done much to dispel the gloomy memories of those poetry recitations. Also, there is Tom Bell himself, who is a regular pick-me-up with his unquenchable cheeriness. The atmosphere is still impregnated with the incense of stale drink and tobacco fumes. Long may it continue thus : without it, Rule's would not have its distinctive cachet.

As has been said, food from the grill is excellent.

* * * * *

The *Lord Belgrave* stands at the corner of Whitcomb Street at the intersection of Panton Street. It is a public-house—serving table d'hôte and à la carte meals in a dining-room upstairs. It specializes in entrecôte steaks. And they are good and cheap.

* * * * *

After a brief sojourn at the Lord Belgrave let's get on a No. 19 or 22 'bus from Piccadilly Circus and donating threepenny fares to the conductor hie ourselves Chelseawards. Alighting—please wait until the 'bus stops—at the King's Picture Playhouse in the King's Road, we can gaze a brief while at the incredibly vivid posters depicting amazing feats of energy and athleticism on the part of galloping cowboys and American policemen. That's the kind of cinema they have here in Chelsea. Having gazed our fill at these examples of advertising art, let's step across the road into the saloon-lounge of yon hostelry trading under the sign of the *Cadogan Arms*.

This hostelry takes pride of place over the Markham and the Rising Sun : other public-houses favoured with the patronage of Chelsea's artists. In olden days, when first I knew it, it flourished mightily under the genial direction of Charles Knight, diamond merchant, and his kindly, hospitable wife, Mrs. Nellie Knight.

A lapse of years, and the Cadogan Arms is now under the management of Mr. and Mrs. Charles Webber—actually, I think, under the management of daughter Doreen, aged two, who has red hair and blue eyes. This young lady is the real boss.

Though there has been a change of ownership, the place still flourishes as of yore, and is still as popular. Not only that, but the majority of the old-time patrons are still here. One face only is missing from among the old crowd, and that is Chiquita's. Chiquita was the Cuban-Mexican-Spanish model for Augustus John. She was the leader of most practical jokes perpetrated in the saloon lounge. Also the originator of that iniquitous game called " Buff ! " Briefly, if a member-Buff let go of his drink even for a moment, any other member could shout " Buff ! " and claim free drinks for all Buffs present. Which accounts to this day for the subconscious habit of many people of grasping their glasses tightly on all occasions.

Augustus John, who lives around the corner from the Cadogan Arms, still comes in sometimes for his " beer in a tankard," which is the correct way to drink that beverage at this public-house.

Always there are other artists, sculptors—the wives,

sweethearts, mistresses and lovers of those same. Were this saloon lounge in the open air, it would be London's nearest approximation to the Quartier Latin. Then there are the models, bless their hearts ! " Broke " one day, flush the next ; always ready to share what they have, if they have it. Diane West is the doyenne of these models. Diane of the large brown eyes and infectious laugh ; who drinks beer from a tankard ; and likes it. Betty Daybell, Alma Tyler, oh ! a score of others who are regular patronnes of the Cadogan Arms. Who, when this place closes at ten o'clock, troop *en masse* to that dreary Bohemian resort called The Chelsea Barn, there to while away another hour or two of the nights that are too long.

Upstairs from the saloon lounge is the billiard room ; it is the marker here who has the duty of shouting " Last orders ! Time, gentlemen, time ! Come along now, please ! "

You can get food here. Plain fare such as cold roast beef and the like : suggest you ask Mrs. Webber, or Kitty, the nice barmaid.

* * * * *

Whilst we are in Chelsea, you might just stop a minute at the famous old public-house called *Six Bells and Bowling Green*. There actually is a very beautiful bowling green at the back of this establishment—the scene of many tournament and championship matches with the " woods and jack."

You can get cheap table d'hôte luncheons in the dining-room upstairs ; and snacks, of a sort, in the huge saloon bar.

* * * * *

By the way, it would be elementary justice to mention the *Chelsea Grill* in *Flood Street*. It is the one star that gleams with a bright light in Chelsea's heaven of burnt-out constellations. You can get a really excellent three-course luncheon here for one shilling and ninepence ; and a table d'hôte dinner for three shillings and sixpence. There is a decorative and imposing wine list, choice from which is gratified by a waiter who scampers to a neighbouring public-house. The Chelsea Grill is operated by a lady who keeps a handsome Pekin Palace dog : both are mighty popular with regular customers. The chef was lured away from the Cavalry Club ; which accounts for the good food.

TAVERNA MEDICEA, 45, *Frith Street*, *W*.1.

Come to think of it, you were promised a further trip to Soho, to do some more browsing in the multitudinous restaurants that somehow or other manage to scratch a living for themselves. Well, that is a promise singularly easy to keep. So we might as well set out on our voyage of exploration with no more luggage than some money and a few bismuth tablets.

Frith Street has more than its fair share of eating-places—so we will wander along here first of all. And, of course, are arrested by the spectacle of the doorman wearing mediæval Florentine garb.

Now usually a doorman wearing fancy dress is as good as an angel with a flaming sword to the majority of diners-out. It keeps people away from a place ; restaurants thus guarded can be sure of not getting a large number of customers who are deterred by the sight of a fantastically-dressed doorman. That is so in my case, at least ; and with many scores of other people who react in the same way.

Finally, and only after many misgivings, I was persuaded to try the place, and allowed myself to be steered past that doorman—dressed like the creatures that visit us in our worse dreams.

Inside the place is all " done up " to be a replica of a Florentine tavern in the days of the Medici. And for the benefit of those who don't know, it would be as well to explain that the Medicis were bankers who then became rulers of Tuscany—who lent out money and were the originators of the " three brass balls " seen hanging outside moneylending establishments of the present day—who, having thriven mightily on lending spondulicks at high rates of interest, became patrons of art ; as many another successful pawnbroker has done since their day. Lorenzo " the Magnificent," who lived from 1448 until 1492, is the best known of the Medici family ; probably because he was the most showy and bombastic.

The history of the Medici people was thumped into me with a ruler many years ago, and enough of it stayed for me to pass on this condensed paragraph.

However, let us return to our muttons.

Taverna Medicea is all Medicean Florentine. The knives and forks are made to comply with such instruments in those days ; though I doubt if forks were any part of table equipment in the Middle Ages. The decorations and lighting arrangements are all conceived to give the tavern effect ; one thing is omitted and for which let us render thanks—the tavern stuffiness. This restaurant is light, cool and airy on warm days ; and pleasantly snug on cold days. Needless to say, the atmosphere of being " pleasantly snug " is more usual.

Taverna Medicea is operated by three people : two Barberis and one Calderoni. Only Mr. A. Barberi do I know at all well. He is a pleasant, dark-haired young man who concerns himself chiefly with the buying and executive side of the business. He is so English, too. More so than many English-born people could ever hope to be. Rides a motor-cycle and plays cricket. Yes ; cricket actually. He has other traits which stamp him as an Anglophile of the most rabid kind. As for his prowess as a cricketer, I cannot speak. Though he confessed that his highest score for last season was a beggarly twenty-six runs. No need to cause anxiety in County Cricket circles.

Signor Calderoni—and please observe that he is given

the Italian prefix !—is, I believe, *chef de cuisine* ; a little dark man with a permanent twinkle in his eye. He hails from Turin, and that, to those who know Turin, is enough reason for anyone to feel good-humoured. Turin not being a particularly amusing or attractive town ; unless your mind has a natural bent for pondering upon ancient monuments. As for the other Barberi—Mr. or Signor—he is a mystery to me.

The Medici arms, of course, are on everything. Salt and pepper shakers, plates, cups, saucers, and it has been rumoured that they are on the underside of each piece of Raviolo. This is to give an air of verisimilitude to the place.

Have you gathered a suggestion of the atmosphere of this place ?

Alas ! there is no dominant personality allowed to pervade Taverna Medicea. Which is a pity ; for all authentic taverns have the impress of a master mind. Especially is this the case with Florentine " dives."

Now, if it is permitted, to diverge for a moment and make a suggestion to Messrs. Barberi and Calderoni. You have at the Taverna a head waiter by name of Abrado. A man of singular tact and charm ; a ready, understanding *maître d'hôtel*. Ask the ladies who patronize your restaurant ! Why not allow the good Abrado more limelight ; give him a freer hand with matters in the dining-room ; in brief, allow his strong and pleasant personality a chance of expression.

He is, I am sure, perfectly capable of looking after the room to the great, good gain of Taverna Medicea.

Another suggestion. There are far too many " commis " about the place. It's all cluttered up with these junior waiters : give a bunch of commis a chance, and they'll idle, waste time, and do a host of small things that all help to give a bad impression. Sack half of them. It'll be no great loss. Make the remainder work hard for their living. It won't kill them ; and will certainly clear the decks somewhat.

The menus were designed by Cricketer Barberi. They are among the most attractive it has been my good fortune to see. Judge for yourself—and you are sure to agree, if you admire woodcuts. This refers, of course, to the outside, front and back of the menu. The inside is designed to appeal to the less æsthetic side of man's composite make-up.

Couvert is sixpence. Which seems an unnecessarily high charge for bread and butter and a napkin. The entire " Lista delle Vivande " is in Italian. Smoked Scotch salmon becomes " Salmone Scozzese Affumicato." So, for some of the items you will require the help of friend Abrado, otherwise you may order who-knows-what if you do not understand Italian.

As a further guide, the specialities of the restaurant are set in italics under the headings or sections. Thus you find *Minestrone alla Casalinga* at one shilling, is so marked out in the soups ; *Frittata alla Contadina* at

two shillings, in the egg section ; *Risotto alla Piemontese*
at one-and-nine ; *Troterelle Cabato* at three shillings.
" Oh ! a veree speshul troud, sir ! " And so on
through the entire list.

Unlike other Soho restaurants, Taverna Medicea is
fully licensed, which eliminates the wine-shop nuisance.
And a great point with Chianti-lovers is, that you can
buy red or white Italian wine by the glass ; have it
poured from a truly Italian flask in a truly Italian
swinging flask-holder ! 'Tis the only swinging flask-
holder I've seen north of Bolzano, Italian Tyrol.

The food is of a sure, steady quality : everything is
cooked properly and well. The service, at present, is
somewhat fumbled by those swarms of commis that
mill around, making a great palaver—and avoiding
anything that looks like a slight job of work.

The following tip is good advice, however. Button-
hole Abrado, and try to win his heart. Maybe it may
not occur to you that he is not a rich man ; the
gratitude and attention of some one not rich can be
won in a simple way . . . in this case, such a method
is to be commended, for it is productive of most
excellent results.

Asking Mr. Barberi for a couple of recipes I was
given two that simply do not figure on the menu !
Now, what can he mean by that ? Is he trying to
promote a couple of new dishes ? So back I dashed
to Taverna Medicea.

" Hey ! Mr. Barberi ! What's this ? "

" Ah—good morning, Mr. Douglas ! Splendid weather ! "

" For cricket you mean ? Yes ; well, I want . . ."

" If it's like this to-morrow, I'll get a game . . ."

" No doubt. What do I care ? I want . . ."

" Oh ! but cricket is a magnificent game ! Why . . ."

" Heavens ! Abrado, good friend ! I want this Risotto con Funghi, and for heaven's sake see that Mr. Barberi doesn't put any cricket balls in it ! "

" Cricket balls ? In risotto ? " said Mr. Barberi. " Why, the idea is out of the question ! " He went. In a day-dream of anticipation.

Abrado attended to my wants and saw to it that plenty of mushrooms were put in the risotto. If you like a risotto with mushrooms, here is the place to get a smooth, mellow and very civilized Italian one. To my mind, such is improved by the addition of peppers cut up and added. Still, that is just a personal prejudice.

Here is the recipe. The price being one shilling and ninepence a portion.

Risotto con Funghi (for six persons).

Ingredients : 1 lb. Italian rice (Novara), 6 oz. fresh butter, 1 small onion, 6 oz. grated cheese, 6 oz. fresh mushrooms, 2 pints chicken broth, salt and pepper.

Mode : Chop up the onion and put into a copper saucepan with 2 oz. of butter. Allow the onion to cook to a golden colour, stirring occasionally with a wooden spatola. Add the sliced mushrooms and allow to cook over a slow fire for a further 5 minutes. Then add the rice and the broth, which should be boiling, stir again and cook over a slow fire for 20 minutes. Remove from the fire, add the rest of the butter and cheese. Serve at once.

Here is a delightful and simple-to-prepare veal recipe. Like the *risotto con funghi*, it does not figure on the menu. Don't let that upset you ; if you have it, you may be sure it will figure on the bill.

Piccata al Marsala (for six persons).

Take 24 very small escallops of veal, dip them in flour and cook them to a golden colour over a quick fire. Drain off the butter and add half a glass of Marsala, a spoonful of good gravy and a piece of butter. Mix the sauce well and serve with mashed potatoes.

Particularly delightful to watch in operation is the weird, prehistoric contraption for grating Parmesan cheese. The instrument, resembling an abortive mill wheel designed by Heath Robinson, does the job most

185

effectively ; it's no use coveting it for use in your own home. For Mr. Barberi watches over that machine like a hen does over a lone chick.

Here at Taverna Medicea one meets our old friend Mortadella di Bologna : the grand-daddy of all sausages. Have a whack at this before the risotto—finish your dinner with a sweet called *Involtino All'Inferno* ! Swig glass after glass of good white wine ; and as you pour from the flask, be sure to spill a few drops on the table-cloth to propitiate the little demons who would jump into the flask itself, an you did not give them their share on the table-cloth.

The keynote of this restaurant is an easy-going friendliness : the service requires slight modifications on the lines suggested : the food is good and very reasonably priced—the wine is well up to standard and there is no hint of extortion in the moderate charges made for it.

In the head waiter, Abrado, is the stuff of which famous *maîtres d'hôtel* are made—given an opportunity.

THE SOHO LINE-UP.

At the Soho Square end of Greek Street there was, until recently, a small restaurant run by Angelo Mainini and Giuseppe Sommariva, one-time waiters at Gennaro's. It has failed after a few months' existence only. I am sorry, for Angelo had been a friend of mine over a period of many years. The premises are still a restaurant and when last I strolled past, were being painted a very spring-like shade of pale green.

Other indicators were, that the new place is to be called *Josef's* ; it is to be " personelly " managed ; it is to specialize in Serbo-Hungarian dishes.

Two doors away is *Au Jardin des Gourmets*. Very good, French, provincial cooking at reasonable prices. The menu and charges are displayed prominently in the window. So you can ruminate thereon and count the change in your pocket and let that be the deciding factor—that is, if cost be any consideration. Be certain that Au Jardin des Gourmets serves excellent food.

Still farther along *Greek Street* we pass *L'Escargot Bienvenu*, of which mention has been made already. Then, turning left into *Old Compton Street*, come to *Beguinot's* restaurant ; more generally known as *Le Diner Français*. This place has a reputation for its table d'hôte luncheon or dinner at two shillings and six-pence. The appearance of the dining-room is reminiscent of an hotel dining-room in any small provincial town in Normandy. Be it said, too, that the food and service are such as you will get in any small French town ; the atmosphere, therefore, being authentic.

The meals read well on the menu, and for the low price it is astonishing to learn that the food is good.

The *Restaurant Brice*, formerly at 17, Old Compton Street, has moved to *Wardour Street*.

Practically next door to Kettner's is a small restaurant called *Le Moulin d'Or* at 27, *Church Street*. Rumour hath it that the food here comes from Kettner's kitchens, but is served at half Kettner's prices. How much truth there may be in this story it is impossible for me to say. It is well worth your while to dine at the Moulin d'Or—and the prices will cause you no great moaning.

Just a stone's throw from here, at Number 12, *Church Street*, is the *Treviglio*, a tiny place with its own clientèle of devoted patrons. Good food and cheap.

In *New Compton Street*, just before you come to Gennaro's, is the *Japanese Restaurant*. Now there may be some people who like food from these islands of the East. People who like to fuss mysteriously with mysterious and unnamable objects over a gas ring on the table. People who like the studiedly casual service of Japanese waiters. This restaurant began by being outrageously expensive, but has now reduced prices so that it is absurdly cheap. You can get a four-course table d'hôte luncheon or dinner here for the ridiculously low sum of two shillings. A meal incorporating genuine Japanese specialities : if you can appreciate such fare. As a slight deviation from this short Soho line-up, it may interest those fanatics of Japanese food, to learn that there is yet another Jap. restaurant that serves precisely the same dishes of the Far East at even lower prices. This place is in a basement in Villiers Street off the Strand.

Although not in Soho proper, the *Restaurant Boulogne* at 27, *Gerrard Street* belongs to the Soho category. It is not so showy as some, but the low prices compensate for this. Needless to say, the cuisine is Gallic in flavour.

There is the *Monte Carlo Restaurant* in *Lisle Street*; almost at the back of the Empire Theatre, whereat one may get a meal that is perfectly satisfactory as regards price and quality. Though there is nothing about the Monte Carlo to cause ravings of excitement. It is unpretentious and satisfies the unexacting needs of large numbers of regular patrons.

In *Whitcomb Street* is the *Genova Restaurant*. A cheap and rather gloomy little Italian place.

At 81, *New Oxford Street* is the *Royal Trocadero Restaurant*.

Yet farther along, and nearly opposite Museum Station, is a superlatively dull-looking place, called *The Museum Restaurant*. By all that's surprising, the food is really good, considering how absurdly cheap every item is. Try the veal escallops here—with them, sauté potatoes and green salad; with the last-named a dressing made at the table by the old, old French waiter who understands such things.

There must be fifty or more restaurants in Soho which never have seen, and never will see, my patronage. There is no reason why anyone should shorten his life unduly by trying all these places. Wardour Street,

Dean Street, Frith Street and Greek Street ; crossed
by Compton Streets, Old and New ; Brewer Street,
Church Street and others. Every alleyway has its restaurant or two. There's the Abyssinian place in Archer
Street ; an exceedingly good Kosher place in Wardour
Street ; a Cyprian café between Dean and Frith
Streets ; two Greek and one Montenegrin restaurants
also, that I have seen but not tried. My good health
is a gift from on High ; I will not abuse it by being
too thorough in my investigations of eating-places of
Soho. They come and they go. As evanescent as soap
bubbles. By the time you read this, there may be some
that are mentioned in this book that have vanished ;
others taken their places ; hired two bay trees in tubs ;
placed an order with the " vol au vent " factory and
started business.

" *Omnia mutantor, nos et mutamur in illis.*"

FARTHER AFIELD.

A feeling of satiety comes upon me. The kind that
causes me to be a nuisance to head waiters. Sugges-
tions of " zometheeng ver' go-o-od and speshyal " leave
me unmoved. Grilled peacocks' tongues on a bed of
iced red caviar surrounded by any fancy fal-lals you
like to imagine, piques me not in the slightest. I
don't want such a dish. Nor anything else that is put
forward for my inspection and proposed delectation.

In short, I am suffering reaction that is inevitable

from too prolonged a bout of London's restaurants ; excellent and varied though they be. That final wallow in Soho set the seal on everything.

The sun shines out and the Great Outdoors is calling. In fact, the English summer has come and who can say for how long that will last ? Avaunt ye, tournedos garnished with weary watercress. I'm off to the country to see rump-steaks, prime ribs of beef and lamb cutlets in the making.

It is fortunate indeed that my yearning for fields of buttercups coincides with an invitation to spend a couple of weeks in the country—doing nothing, save only to amuse myself. A car, of sorts, which I can use at any old time of the day or night ; answerable to nobody, not even my host and hostess as to where I might drive. Now that was an invitation after my own heart.

Would I accept ? Within ten minutes of receiving the letter of invitation, I was on my way.

For three days the time was spent pleasantly enough in studying the few facial expressions of cows, geese and the like ; watching a Sealyham scratch fleas ; timing snails as they whizzed across a flagged garden path. Fortified mightily by such displays of energy on the part of Nature's more humble forms of life, I accepted my host's offer of the car and spent some days in pottering.

Now in the whole world there's no more pleasant

191

district for pottering than in a field of territory of fifty miles' radius from Hyde Park Corner. Look at any road map and see for yourself. Main arterial roads ; highways ; narrow country lanes ; the Chilterns ; North and South Downs ; common lands ; dozens of old-world villages ; the sea-coast ; everything possible in the way of typical English countryside within fifty miles of Hyde Park Corner—that rendezvous for Guardsmen and nursemaids.

Thus idly I ambled hither and yon ; playing that game of taking the first road right and then the first left, just to see where such course would lead me. During my perambulating I visited dozens of hostelries of all species for this, that or the other kind of refreshment.

Most of them well known to the motoring fraternity ; some not so widely known. Some undeservedly popular on account of tradition or non-maintained reputation. Others, as yet, most excellent and deserving of the greatest praise. Such a one is the World's End at Cobham, of which I have made mention earlier in this book.

In this chapter I will set forth record of a round score. Make your own deductions as to what may be the merits and demerits of such and such a place. Then if you still feel unconvinced, beg, borrow or steal a car and sally forth to confirm or refute your own deductions.

You know the Kingston By-Pass ? If so, you will have seen, and patronized mayhap, the *Ace of Spades Roadhouse* which is at a cross-roads. This place is astounding by reason of its rapid and continuous growth. Aladdin's Palace is a mere amateur by comparison with the Ace of Spades. Originally it started with being a filling station. Then, by knocking a few garage boxes into one room, the first elementary restaurant was begun. Progress after that was phenomenal ; day and night service for car supplies, repairs, food, and so forth ; then came the building of bigger and more bee-yutiful premises ; chiefly from timbers taken from barns known to be at least four hundred years old. Bakeries for home-made cakes and bread. A floor laid for dancing and the engagement of a small dance band. Radio and gramophone music when wanted or needed.

When last I saw Mr. Hersey, he was grappling with a triple problem—quadruple, rather. Installation of a central heating system ; refrigerating plant ; extension of premises ; construction of a diving pool complete with bathing tents, and big marquee for outdoor dancing. Mr. Hersey is manager of the place. He and his brother run the roadhouse and its equally-famous sister place on the Great West Road at Hounslow.

Just to lighten this burden, I asked :

" How many gallons of petrol do you sell from your two places ? "

" Three-quarters of a million gallons a year," was the prompt answer. " What d'you think of this diving pool ? "

" I think it's too small."

" Yes—well, we are putting in a full-size swimming pool at our Great West Road place, so you can go to whichever one you like. Or you can go some place quite different."

" Thanks. But I'm a customer here."

" Have you paid your bill yet ? " asked Mr. Hersey.

" No."

" In that case, you'd better not go to . . . well, anywhere else ; at least, not until you have settled up."

After which rapid exchange of feeble repartee, Mr. Hersey and his brother—he is Mr. Hersey also—showed me around. They are justifiably proud of everything. Yet, somewhat bewildered at the speed with which things happen.

" We started out as Civil Engineers," explained Mr. Hersey—perhaps it was the other Mr. Hersey—" then we became automobile experts. After that, garage proprietors ; then owners of a filling-station selling our own brand of oils and petrols. Now we have a restaurant business to look after as well as all the other things."

I saw the bakery. Inspected a large brown hole in the ground which was the embryo diving pool. Poked my nose into the automobile repair shops.

Concerning the restaurant, you can lunch, tea, dine, sup or breakfast, in glass-enclosed verandas on either ground or first floor. You can have breakfast at four o'clock in the afternoon, or afternoon tea at two o'clock in the morning. You can order any extraordinary combination of dishes from the menu for your meal, but you won't upset the staff in so doing. The dance floor is upstairs and the hours and charges for that are as follows :

	Minimum charge per person.	Extra for dancing.	Dinner dance.
	s. d.	s. d.	s. d.
Week days 4 p.m. to 6 p.m. . .	Nil	Nil	—
Week days 8 p.m. to midnight . .	2 0	3 0	6 0
Extension nights 8 p.m. to 2 a.m. .	2 0	4 0	7 6
Saturdays 4 p.m. to 6 p.m. . . .	1 6	1 0	—
Saturdays 8 p.m. to midnight . .	3 0	4 0	7 6

The music is dispersed by Vic Filmer's Murray's Club Band.

Here are a few items picked out from an à la carte menu :

	s.	d.
Thick Oxtail Soup . .	1	0
Cream of Tomato . . .	1	0
Escallop of Veal Milanaise .	2	0
Mashed Potatoes . . .	0	6
Prunes and Cream . . .	1	0
Fruit Salad and Cream . .	1	3

Naturally the night menu is rather more expensive. One expects it.

There is a Soda Fountain, too ; I nearly forgot about that. And a special Cold Buffet menu.

Also, during licensed hours, you can get all manner of alcoholic drinks brought in from a neighbouring hostelry. There is a wine list—short but fairly representative—from which you can make your choice of alcoholic refreshment, and the prices are somewhat lower than you will pay in Soho.

Mr. Hersey says that he makes no profit at all on the drinks ; that he prints and pays for the Wine List himself ; employs and pays extra staff for fulfilling orders—yet has no " arrangement " with the publican.

Without reservation this is the place to go to for eggs and bacon with coffee and toast at about three o'clock in the morning. As you will learn, roadhouses cater to all and sundry ; while you have no bias against the " all," you will have to accept and then ignore the " sundry."

As for making use of the Lilliputian diving pool—why, a thirsty elephant could drink its contents in ten minutes. Home-made bread? Excellent, especially as a change from the unvarying perfection and monotonous sameness of machine-baked bread. Car repairs at the Ace of Spades are executed expeditiously and well : which accounts for the charges.

You might try it some fine night ; preferably not during the week-end, when the Ace of Spades is jammed tight with people.

Through some of the most tortuous roads of London —by which I mean those on the south side of Father Thames—we come, eventually, to a road known as Purley Way. Along here is Croydon Aerodrome ; the chief airport for London ; the roosting-place of those giant Imperial Airways machines. The reason for it being called Croydon Aerodrome is that it is located in Purley Way which by-passes the town of Croydon.

The place is very important. Hangars, Customs sheds, Royal Mail depot ; repair shops, garages and a fairly new *Aerodrome Hotel*.

In the early days of this hotel it was my wont to proceed thither by car on a warm summer's afternoon ; take tea on the umbrella'd balcony or the veranda and watch the planes come and go.

The actual meal itself was well below the average so far as quality was concerned ; the fun lay in watch-

ing people arrive by air from all parts of Europe.
Planes of French, Swiss, German and Dutch registra-
tion flitted hither and yon.

There was an added zest to guessing the nationality
of a plane bearing " a banner of strange device."

It is pleasant to record that since those pioneer days
there have been improvements in the food at the Aerodrome Hotel. It is hard to believe that the proximity
of airplanes and all that is thereby implied could
account for the strangeness of flavour, the staleness
and the general state of hopelessness evinced by the
comestibles so sold as being eatable. Eatable they
were ; only just. Now all that is altered ; and the
quality is such that not even the most captious could
find fault.

*　　*　　*　　*　　*

In my potterings I came to *Gibb's Hatch*, Cranleigh,
Surrey. Drop in there, some time. The *Clock House*
and *Cedar Tea-Rooms*, both at Ripley, Surrey, and both
exceedingly well known for teas, home-made cakes 'n'
all that. *The Watermill* just outside Dorking. *Pitt's
Cottage*, Westerham, Kent. *The Old Barn*, Hilden-
borough, Kent. The *Punch Bowl* at Horsham and the
Punch Bowl at Crawley ; at one or both of which Oliver
Cromwell or some one or other slept, or didn't sleep
or something or other, sometime or other. The cakes
are good and served well in most attractive surroundings.

The Mitre at Hampton Court is the Mecca of all those who have spent several hours looking at acres of tapestry in Hampton Court Palace ; losing themselves in the Maze ; paying homage to the Royal Vine ; or admiring the whole palace and gardens of that astute cleric, Cardinal Wolsey. He knew a thing or two, this prelate ; Hampton Court Palace was a good trip from London—and from Henry VIII—in those days.

Just say *Skindles* to the majority of English people and that is sufficient address. This hotel on the river at Maidenhead has acquired a reputation on which it thrives and does a flourishing business. It will give me much pleasure to poke a little gentle fun at Skindles ; and to do so, will make use of their brochure (illustrated). The first sentence in this booklet : " Skindles is unique among hotels, for it has a reputation extending throughout the whole of the English-speaking world." But why and how has it got a reputation ? And for what ? Ah ! Sweet mystery. . . .

" Under the name of the Orkney Arms, this place was the venue for the merrymaking of Charles II and Nell Gwynne." I like " merrymaking." Such a coy word in this case.

" Skindles' popularity as a week-end resort is proverbial." Merrymaking ?

" Visitors without luggage or with handbags only will be required to pay a deposit." Merrymaking ?

I should like to have the monopoly of the " fires in

bedroom " business. Skindles charge five shillings a
day for this necessity ; brought about by the place
being so out of date as to have no central heating.
This is 1933.

Baths :		*s.*	*d.*
Hot, in bathroom .	.	1	0
Cold, in bathroom .	.	1	0

There's no mention of the tariffs for baths, hot or
cold, if taken in the kitchen or public dining-room.

At last, I have found the peak of snobbery. This is
another quotation from the booklet :

" Boulter's Lock has been pictured and described so
often that we need only say it is quite close to
Skindles."

There now, Boulter's Lock ! Don't you feel
honoured at being allowed to be quite close to such
an aristocratic venue for merrymaking ?

There is a reproduction of " A Corner of the Smoke
Room " drawn by Tom W. Aimes. What appeals to
me is the display of bottles at the right of the draw-
ing ; such a gentle hint as to where you may find
the bar ; an excellent and well-stocked bar it is,
too.

The three things of Skindles that appeal to me are :
one, tea on the lawn ; two, the old, old waiters ;
three, the old, old Sealyham terrier. The lawn is perhaps one of the most beautiful hotel lawns in England ;

and that's saying something. Emerald grass, close-clipped like a deep pile velvet carpet under the big shady trees. The lawn slopes gently to the river—a thoroughfare for punts, electric canoes and dignified, haughty swans. The waiters . . . well, if Skindles ever employed men who were not qualified to be grandfathers, then it would lose half of its appeal. The Sealyham terrier is a gentleman of ingrained surliness who accords guests a grudging civility on the score of business ; otherwise, you could go some place else for all he would care.

Skindles is very English indeed. The only possible time for you to go there is mid-week. On other days the place is swamped with specimens of the motoring fraternity to whom one would not entrust the job of polishing a windscreen even. Riff-raff ; and Skindles knows it, but cannot do anything about it.

Why not go and merrymake ?

* * * * *

The *Burford Bridge Hotel* is on the Dorking-Reigate road ; yes, Surrey again. The place is a cross between the Ace of Spades and Skindles without the " popular appeal " features of either ; it has a cachet that places it in a group by itself.

* * * * *

With a rush we get to the north side of London. On the Watford By-Pass is a café restaurant called *The Spider's Web*. This place inaugurated a motor-cycle squad to get alcoholic beverages from the nearest public-house for those eating food in the café. A novel form of service which earned them considerable publicity. It is notable that the rest of the service is as quick-firing as the motor-cycles. The food is as good as the drink brought by these wheeled messengers of Mercury.

* * * * *

Great Fosters at Egham is a lovely Elizabethan house converted into an hotel-restaurant with many other amenities, including a swimming pool. Yet, dining here, I cannot help but feel the reproachful glances of dead-and-gone gallants as, from the spirit world, they see the sad changes that have come upon such a wonderful old place as Great Fosters. All in the name of Progress and Modernity. Maybe I'm too sensitive about this particular resort. Then I knew Great Fosters in the far-off days. . . .

* * * * *

Some years ago, returning from an extended motoring trip on the Continent, winding up with an all-night and day drive across France, I tumbled thankfully into a berth on the Dieppe-Newhaven packet boat and slept. I awoke in the early morning as the boat lay alongside an English quayside. It was late spring. A perfect day. The scent of the Sussex countryside coming in through the open portholes was too much. Up I jumped, dressed and, without thought of shaving, was on deck in a few minutes. My car had been unloaded. No need for further delay. Except to watch for a few minutes the unloading of heavy bars of silver bullion and smile at the jokes made by the good-natured labourers handling these bars as casually as though they were bricks ; under the supervision of one young, unarmed, uninterested policeman.

At seven o'clock I had " cleared " the car and was once again driving on the left-hand side of the road.

Passing through East Grinstead, I was shortly greeted by the most delicious smell in the world. A blend of wallflowers, warm earth, frying bacon and coffee. It was impossible to pass it by, and so, dishevelled as I was, pulled into the front yard of the pseudo-Tudor place called *Ye Olde Felbridge Hotel*.

What a typically English welcome they gave me here. Of course I could have breakfast. Porridge with brown sugar and thick cream ; then there was a choice of haddock or kippers ; eggs and bacon ; grilled ham ; cold buffet ; toast, butter and marmalade ; tea or coffee. Served in a low-ceilinged airy dining-room, looking out upon a profusion of flowers.

Thank God ! Some typical English " military gents " who propped their papers against tea and coffee pots ; and glared at me as though I had intruded upon the intimacies of their toilets. Thus I knew it was a genuine English country hotel—" du premier ordre."

Somewhere near is a golf course ; the reason for many people being here. Even nearer than that attraction are tame-wild rabbits, which hop about the lawn sharing in the domestic life with an old cocker spaniel, hens and a gardener or two. It would cause me no qualms or misgivings if I saw rabbit pie figuring on the menu—I don't eat that English dish at any time.

Subsequent visits for luncheon, tea and dinner confirmed my first impression that Ye Olde Felbridge Hotel of East Grinstead is an undeniably attractive place. Make a note of it, and if you don't find it as pleasant as I have said, then it would be difficult to find the right door at which to lay the blame.

* * * * *

The *White Lion Hotel* at Cobham promises much from its warm, friendly exterior. But the promise is not altogether fulfilled ; inside it's a curious place of the days when conveniences were non-existent, so that nowadays modern conveniences have to be put in very inconvenient places ; as you will learn if you go to this hotel. There is a bar parlour which reminds one somewhat of furniture shops in the Tottenham Court Road. The prices charged seem somewhat high, but the food is good ; above the average.

One Sunday evening, I observed the kitchen chimney blazing away right merrily. So at inconvenience to

myself, sought out Mr. Taylor, the proprietor, and
told him of it. He swore lustily at the chimney and
dashed off to prevent a serious conflagration. Have
seen Mr. Taylor many a time and oft since then, but
not once has he referred in any way to this service.
Which seems rather strange.

Hearty British meals served with a bang is the guid-
ing spirit of the White Lion Hotel. The drinkables
are well above the usual run stocked by country hotels,
for Mr. Taylor has laid in extensive supplies of wines,
spirits and liqueurs to cater to the many and varied
demands of modern motorists. Which is all to the
public good.

*   *   *   *   *

The *Talbot Hotel* at Ripley is one of the slightly-
modernized coaching inns. Very good to regard ; for
which purpose a post-card serves excellently. The
food is solid and satisfying without being wildly exciting. One dines in a room ornamented with muskets
and the like—the illumination being by candles : the
nicest of all lighting by which to dine.

*   *   *   *   *

It would be too much of a tax upon my memory to
state accurately whether the *Old Bell* at Hurley is pre-
William the Conqueror or a mere, beggarly, jumped-
up, twelfth-century inn. Of one thing I am certain.
The Old Bell was in existence, and had been for quite

a respectable number of years, before Cristoforo
Colombo made his momentous and historical West-
bound voyage.

It is still old-world in the sense that hot water is
brought in brass cans to your room upon your arrival.
There is a candlestick by your bedside for the wee sma'
hours, should you be awake and desiring the comfort of
light. Food and drink are expensive and rightly so,
for the cooking is of a high order and the cellar most
extensive.

There is a pleasant garden wherein one may dally
awhile ; there is a garage worthy of your note, too.
Just a huge, old barn redolent of generations of cows
and horses ; a pleasantly pungent smell.

The village of Hurley has been awakened from its
centuries of slumber by the motor traffic which has
sought out and, to some extent, popularized the Old
Bell. Still, should you have a lazy day before you,
stroll about the village or hire a punt or canoe from
the hotel and idle along the diminished Thames.

When I was last there, the Old Bell was operated
by—I think—Captain Taylor. Long may he continue
to flourish and prosper, for he is a charming and courteous host, who studies the comfort and welfare of his
guests.

* * * * *

The *Cedar House* at Cobham. The *Peggy Bedford* on
the road to Staines ; its actual address being Colne-

brook, a village now " by-passed." Take my tip, and by-pass this by-pass. For the old, straggling village will repay a few minutes of your time.

The *Brent Bridge Hotel* only just outside London and to the north is the progenitor of English roadhouses. It has lovely gardens, with artificial lakes. A putting course. Veranda dining-rooms. Ballroom, wherein one dances to a fairly good dance band. The Brent Bridge Hotel has all the potentialities of being a first-rate, first-class roadhouse. Everything is cheap, and hence it is exceedingly popular, being but forty minutes' drive from Piccadilly Circus.

This is just a rough survey of a few of the hundreds of restaurants, cafés, hotels and so forth around London.

My failure to include many others of equal or greater repute is not to be taken as being an intentional slight on my part. Simply that I did not happen to visit them during my two weeks' holiday from London.

The county of Kent is full of attractive places.

" Up the river " is synonymous with places of refreshment and entertainment. Who does not know the *Hotel de Paris* at Bray ? *Phyllis Court* . . . *Hungaria River Club* . . .?

Not having been to any of these places within recent months, I cannot say how good they are or how bad —in my opinion. That they still do business is proof enough that they enjoy a considerable patronage. Good luck to them.

It's time we were back in London. Jump into car or train and let's see what that frowsy, untidy old woman can offer to our reinvigorated palates.

"PUB CRAWL."

Even a couple of weeks away from town, and London looks a place of enchantment. It is the same thing if one is away from it for longer periods than that.

London is a good place to leave ; it's equally inspiring to come back to it.

Let's have a drink or two to celebrate the return of the prodigal.

Finch's—"Wines from the Wood"—is the first place. Now, there are many branches of this firm. The one that enjoys my intermittent custom is that in the Strand ; there's a good reason for my preference. For, after a couple of excellent pale sherries, *chez* Finch I can teeter across the road to *Short's* and repeat the performance.

For some unknown reason, after two sherries at Finch's chased by a couple of drinks at Short's, I feel inspired to send transatlantic cables from Marconi House ; just because it's next door to Short's, maybe.

From Short's, the next step, or steps rather, is to proceed westward as far as the American bar of the

Tricity, where I lap up a couple of properly-iced cocktails served by a very haughty lady.

By this time it should be impressed upon the mentality that one is in London.

Still going along the Strand, there is *Romano's*; the
bar of the *Tivoli Cinema*, and that dreary dive called
the *Bodega* in Bedford Street. The last-named is much
patronized by Thespians and other wearers of imitation
Persian lamb coat-collars. It's easy enough to differ-
entiate between the actors and " the others." " The
others " will not try to cadge free drinks from you.

If, by now, you discover you are short a few members of your party, there is only one thing to do. Back
track as far as *Henekey's* or *Patmac's Coal Hole* and
rout out the missing. You may even find some have
wandered up a narrow alleyway and are drinking beer
at the *Peacock* in Maiden Lane.

Let's see . . . where were we? Oh yes. The
Bodega. Quash firmly any suggestion of going to the
bar in Charing Cross Station. It's too melancholy a
procedure to drink in an atmosphere of Departure and
Arrival.

Some may want to go to the *Grand Hotel* bar;
others to the *Chandos*. There's only one thing to do:
compromise by going to both.

By this time, you will be convinced that nowhere in
the world is there such a gay town as London. Weav-
ing your way to Leicester Square, snatch a " quick 'un "

at the *Café Anglais* ; " the other half " at the *Lord Belgrave* ; " the odd one " at *L'Apertif* in *Lyons' Corner House*—then, by all that's astounding you find yourself standing up at the *Trocadero Long Bar*. The bar is for " gentlemen only."

Ruminating upon this and that, it behoves us to steer a zigzag course across Shaftesbury Avenue to the *Monico* bar.

Then there are three brasseries to be visited. In each one a large lager has to be drunk. *The Monico ; Oddy's* and the *Café Royal* brasserie.

By this time, the bright idea will occur to some convivial soul that the party ought to go farther afield and again work its way back to the West End. Such a scheme is sure to be hailed with shouts of acclamation. So, chartering taxi-cabs, the next port of call is the *Clarendon* at Hammersmith. In obedience to the homing instinct, there is then the Kensington Cinema bar, and after that the *Goat* in Kensington High Street. This is the tavern which has a sign warning the thirsty wayfarer that it is a mile and a quarter to the next house of refreshment.

Even London taxis can cover that distance in about fifteen minutes, and so the *Premier Lounge* in Dover Street is next visited by the " party of gents with hollow legs " as the taxi-drivers referred to their fares.

And, of course, just across the road is Sam in Hatchett's bar. " Dear ole Sham ? Mushn't forge'

Sham ! " Sam is duly honoured with our presence.
Then Jeanne and Scottie at Hatchett's other bar ; yes,
the other bar !

Finally, we are poured down the stairs of the
Brasserie Universelle in Piccadilly Circus. Let me
collect my scattered wits and tell you of this place.
It is underground ; 'neath the Criterion Theatre ; it
is large and cavernous ; it is on two levels at that, of
which the lower one is devoted to tables for eating and
drinking, and the upper level is devoted to tables for
drinking and drinking. It specializes in cheap food
of the Welsh rarebit type ; though the menu is long
and varied enough to suit most people. The place is
pseudo-Teutonic, an affectation helped materially by
employing a few Prussian waiters. There is a band ;
on my last visit there it consisted of four women with
dance band instruments.

If you like cheap food that is definitely palatable and
lager beer that is properly iced then the Brasserie Universelle is deserving of a visit from you.

If, after a pub crawl on the lines I have suggested,
you are still able to walk without a too-definitely un-
steady gait, then pay a visit to the *Machlachan*, which
lies in an inconspicuous alleyway behind Fleet Street.
Here will be gathered together certain members of the
scribbling fraternity. It is a safe bet that at least two
men in the bar are in a state of glassy-eyed beatifica-
tion. Don't think, from that remark, that journalists

are always drunk. There's a rule governing such matters. The rule is, a journalist is only drunk when some one else can afford it.

Have a drink in the Public Bar of the *Rising Sun* in Cheyne Walk. Drop in, *en route*, at the *Stanley Arms* in Gloucester Road. Explain to me, if you can, why that sedate family hostelry, *Bailey's Hotel* opposite Gloucester Road Station, should have such unusually fine sherry.

There is the *Green Man* at the Regent's Park end of Great Portland Street. The *Cranleigh* in Fulham Road—the saloon bar entrance being *en face de* Sydney Street.

The *Spaniards' Inn* on Hampstead Heath. The setting of many an uproarious jollification. " *Charlie's* " down in the East End ; any taxi-driver knows that place.

The *Windsor Castle* by Victoria Station ; much patronized by ranking and non-commissioned members of His Majesty's land forces. And in justice to many a short drink, I must make mention of the *Wellington* in Waterloo Road. The proximity of this place to the Union Jack Club ensures an excellent patronage from representatives of His Majesty's Navy, Army and Air Force. The Union Jack Club . . . ah me ! Yes.

If you feel like being slightly more elegant, then scurry back to the West End and have a drink at the

Criterion. Pop around the corner and have another one in *Rayner's*. Better have a lobster salad here; they are good and cheap.

Should you feel enterprising, have a strong drink at that transpontine focal centre the *Elephant and Castle*. It's a famous place in the South of London.

Then if, after a visit to all these places, you are still in full possession of your faculties, you are a better man than I am. On the other hand, should you be feeling slightly muzzy, fuzzy or wuzzy, there is an excellent suggestion I would like to make. Hie ye with all speed to the Turkish Baths—open day and night— in Jermyn Street and be strong-minded with yourself. A really good Turkish Bath, followed by a cold plunge; an eau-de-Cologne friction *et al*; then Turkish Bath tea served to you in your Turkish Bath cubicle and you'll sleep the innocent dreamless sleep of the thoroughly wicked. In the morning you will awaken with sufficient strength to meander feebly to Perkin's the chemists in Piccadilly and drink one of their famous pick-me-ups.

Such a pub crawl followed up by the Turkish Bath and so forth is almost guaranteed to make you forswear alcoholic beverages for at least a week.

I am certain that my hand could be guided along any signature line the Blue Ribbon League might wish to place before me. That is, if I were crazy enough to follow out a plan of pub-crawling outlined for your

over-indulgence ; not for mine. I tread a well-trod
path when it comes to drinking. Any place more than
one hundred yards from Eros knows me not ; and
precious few within that radius.

*   *   *   *   *

Now, there is in London a host of very-English restaurants. Places with the tradition of years behind
them.

For as long as possible I avoided going to them ;
that is, from the standpoint of this catalogue of mine.
These restaurants bored me in " the good old days "
when I did go to them occasionally. The idea of visiting them in a semi-professional capacity was more than
I had bargained for. Hence, many famous names
figure in this brief recapitulation. Yes ; I've been to
them all again—and see no reason to change my former
opinion of them. They are not hectically exciting restaurants ; and though the cuisine in most cases is excellent, yet there is a deadly dullness about such
places. A dullness that could not be mitigated by the
most Lucullan of banquets.

So I shall gabble through a list of names—to satisfy
first, myself ; second, my conscience ; and third, to
forestall any reader's comment to the effect, " You've
never been to such-and-such restaurant." Well, here
you are ; you can be assured that I have been to all of
them. And to a good many more such-and-such restaurants the memory of which is so dreadful that it

214

would be an imposition upon the public to perpetuate in print the names of such poison-palaces.

Only the excellent, the good and the tolerable find mention in this Martyr's Litany.

The *Café Royal* in *Regent Street*. Elegant, smart, expensive ; changed out of all recognition from the old Café Royal of Bohemian days. Food is superb and the service beyond reproach—but you have to pay for it and pay thoroughly. The popularity of this restaurant is proof enough that the high prices are justified. Try an example of the chef's " paper bag " cooking, such as roast chicken.

Oddenino's also in *Regent Street*. Dear old Oddy's. Yes ; dear old Oddy's. A good place. I would call to your attention the lager beer imported direct from Pilsen.

The Monico in *Shaftesbury Avenue*. Has a string orchestra perched in a Musicians' Gallery. At times this orchestra gets really frivolous and plays foxtrots not more than five years old. The Monico has the distinction of being the place where I first struggled with artichoke and Hollandaise sauce. Incidentally, the rest of the cooking is very good. Here is something you might try when September 1st brings in that excellent morsel, the partridge. " *Perdreau Monico.*" Just a baby bird stuffed with rice, foie gras and truffles. Delicious.

Frascati's in *Oxford Street* has its ups and downs.

Twenty years ago, when I first went there, was one of the " ups." Twenty years ago sounds a long time ! I hasten to add, it was the first time I had been taken to a late dinner—and then by Mrs. Muriel Draper, who wrote " Music at Midnight." When next I visited Frascati's it was, without doubt, the most dreary restaurant in the world. Now the cycle is complete and again it is light and gay. A hectic, feverish flush is in the wizened cheeks of this old dame, Frascati. She's getting away with the bluff, though. There are two things with which I associate this place. The first is, that peculiar dish—fruit or vegetable, —heart of palm. The second, those strange, brown aromatic Cyprian cigarettes with the wooden tips.

They have excellent cooking here. The place is somewhat frightening ; it's so darned huge.

The *Holborn Restaurant*—in Holborn, of course—is the venue of Club Luncheons ; Lodge Banquets, and . . . there's no need to dilate further, other than to say the Holborn is really English.

Pagani's in *Great Portland Street*. Italian, French, English—Heaven knows what nationality this restaurant is not. Like a clever courtesan, Pagani's is all things to all men. No mean feat, either. Excellent coffee, such as you do not find in an English restaurant. Steak, kidney, lark and mushroom pie—such as you can find only in the most ultra-English place. Wiener Schnitzel that would do justice to a Viennese chef.

216

What is one to deduce from such little cosmopolitanisms ? And the Italian name !

Gatti's at 436, *Strand*. Ask an old-time habitué for his opinion. But be prepared for a long, eulogistic discourse about Gatti's.

The *Coventry Restaurant* in *Rupert Street* makes a big song and dance of its table d'hôte luncheons and dinners. As such meals go, they are exceedingly good value for money. A luncheon at three shillings and dinner at four-and-six is far from excessive. You can feed à la carte also.

The *Florence* is opposite. Specializes in table d'hôte meals, also. Quick service and quite good cooking.

Reggiori's is at 1, *Euston Road*, *N.W.*1. The simplicity of the address is equalled by the simple goodness of the cooking ; decidedly cheap.

Pinoli Restaurant is at 17, *Wardour Street*, *W.*1. I hold no brief either for or against Pinoli's. Any invitation to luncheon there will not set my heart a-flutter with excitement.

Snow's Chop House at 3, *Sherwood Street*, by the Regent Palace Hotel, is one of those old places that has sawdust on the floor. The purpose of this is unknown to me ; and abhorrent also. There is a good selection of things to choose from the grill and everything is very reasonable in price.

Queen's Restaurant is in *Sloane Square*. Has a good cuisine and service. Good, but very dull, however.

And the same applies to the *Kensington Restaurant* which is in *Church Street* opposite St. Mary Abbott's.

The *Ivy Restaurant* is at 1, *West Street*, opposite the Ambassador's Theatre. It is much patronized by those who have reached the higher flights in the theatrical profession. Also those sweet young things of the chorus who can persuade a sufficiently affluent swain to take them there. For the Ivy is the favoured restaurant of many dramatists, managers and others who have the " say-so " in casting theatrical productions.

Considering the really excellent quality of the food the prices are far from excessive. One of the specialities of this place is *Sole Bonne Femme*. Have it : it's good. Two people can dine and wine here most excellently for a sum total of twenty-five shillings ; provided you be content with Sauterne to drink. For that price you get a dinner to include such items as the Sole Bonne Femme to follow grape fruit ; tournedos which are as juicy as I like them—and that's a high standard, incidentally ; the necessary vegetables ; another pet dish of the Ivy Restaurant, which is Soufflé en Surprise ; coffee ; couvert. So you have no kick coming to you on the score that you are overcharged when they give you a dinner like that.

ASTORIA DANCE SALON, *Charing Cross Road, W.*1.

When it comes to a matter of dancing, maybe I'm not the best authority. On being asked where to go, it is easy to give the name of a big hotel where there is a good dance band. You see, I'm not so very fond of dancing. Some years ago—quite a number of years ago, in fact—I used to run dance bands for a living. Even played in one of them myself on occasions. That gave me a new slant from which to view the Terpsichorean art as practised on the ballroom floor. The more I see of the average person's dancing, the more convinced do I become that the Vernon Castles of this world are mighty few and far between.

Gradually, and with one excuse or another, I've managed to ease myself out of any dance engagements wherein I might be expected to take an active part on the floor. It's more fun, to my way of thinking, to sit on the side lines and let others contort their bodies for my amused edification. Dance music appeals to me. The only use I have for the " wahless " in this country is between 10.35 p.m. and midnight.

Nevertheless, from a strong sense of duty, I set out, complete with partner, to find some place whereat one may dance most cheaply, yet to a good band ; on a good floor and amid surroundings not too unpleasant.

It was a warm afternoon and I had taken the sly precaution of wearing shoes that were blessed with thin rubber soles ; such as would preclude any dancing on my part.

Thus we arrived at the Astoria Dancing Salon, which is underneath the cinema of that name in Charing Cross Road. Near to the site once occupied by Rector's night club.

Half a crown a person was the charge made for a session of dancing from three o'clock until six o'clock in the afternoon. That price includes also a table d'hôte tea.

Complete with four tickets, two of which admitted us to the arena—I mean, Salon—we took our place at a corner table ; and handed over the other tickets to a " bunionated " waitress, in exchange for our tea.

I was agreeably surprised. The dance place is octagonal in shape ; there is plenty of floor space ; tables around the bull-ring and on the gallery that runs all around. The lighting arrangements are good and effective. Soft without being of that lurid, naughty-naughty suggestiveness so much a part of certain City tea-rooms I could name.

The waitress staggered back to our table 'neath the weight of a teapot big enough to satisfy the wants of ten people ; the water jug was a match for it. Toasted buns, bits of sandwiches and a small selection of quite impossible, sticky cakes.

The music is quite satisfactory without being of the

nature to make you delirious with desire to dance. If you do get up and cavort, a perfectly satisfactory " beat " is maintained for you. The Romany Band and the Melodians take turns in catering to the patrons' needs in the way of musical rhythm.

Evening dance sessions are from eight o'clock until midnight and the price is three shillings and six-pence.

If you want to dance with your sister, or you cannot afford to take " the girl friend " to a more expensive place, then the Astoria is for such as you. That it meets with and supplies a long-felt want is evident enough from the numbers of people who patronize the Astoria at both the afternoon and evening sessions. The standard of dancing is high ; these patrons, the regular ones that is, are as full of rhythm as can be. So go prepared to do your best—for the sake of your partners.

STRAND PALACE HOTEL.

Really it is too preposterous. Here I am compelled to give yet more gratuitous publicity to J. Lyons & Co., Ltd. It seems that not only have they a finger in most of England's wholesale catering, but that they own half of London into the bargain ; they and the Duke of Westminster between them.

An American friend of mine elected to stay at the Strand Palace Hotel ; he'd " read somewhere or other it was a pretty good joint." As he was visiting my home town, it was up to me to call on him, so that he could take me to the Tower of London; show me Westminster Abbey and so on. When in New York, I'll take him to the top of the Empire State Building and also on a round of speakeasies.

" We'll lunch here," he said. And he meant right in the hotel; whereat I groaned inwardly. For I was assailed by thoughts of " Roast Beef—9d. ; Yorkshire Pud.—1d. extra."

Because he was an American, my friend was full of facts about the Strand Palace Hotel. It has 900 bed-rooms—the only hotel in Europe that is bigger being the Regent Palace with 1,050 bedrooms. I still possess the menu on which he scribbled that harrowing piece of vital information. Through splodges of Worcester-shire Sauce—maybe it's Heinz' Ketchup—I can decipher items dealing with air-washers ; no bells in hotel, all light signs ; manufactured weather ; humidifiers ; washing-up plant deals with 120,000 pieces an hour. A maze of statistical information. Now, how can such matters be of interest to my friend who happens to be a ballistic expert ?

I might have saved my groans, for we had the table d'hôte luncheon of the day. It was exceedingly good too, eaten in the Grill Room whence " the air is ex-hausted every three minutes by means of large fans in the roof. These fans remove 285 tons of air an hour."

I, too, can quote figures if I'm given a chance to see the hotel manager.

Here is the menu.

Hors-d'Œuvre à la Grecque

or

Grape Fruit en Coupe

or

Thick Ox-Tail.

———

Œuf Poché Froid à la russe

or

Devilled Whitebait

or

Grilled Codling Niçoise.

———

Calf's Liver Chasseur

or

Roast Pork and Apple Sauce.
Flageolets Fines Herbes.
Pommes Rissolées

or

Le Buffet-Froid (au Choix).
Roast Beef. Ham. Brawn.
Pressed Beef. Roast Lamb. Veal and Ham Pie.
Salade Verte.

———

Rhubarb Tart and Custard

or

Orange or Vanilla Ice

or

Fruit.

223

I had the thick ox-tail soup, which was not terribly good, as it came in a cold plate. Cold poached egg " a la russe "—an interesting snack ; roast pork and the " fixings " and finished with rhubarb tart with vanilla ice : a combination sweet which upset the waiters for a moment.

Although I was a guest I managed to sneak a look at the bill. The table d'hôte luncheon is three shillings per person, which is cheap. There was nothing niggardly in the portions set before me. For which I was truly thankful, as the large meal induced a pleasant state of coma. This acted as a breakwater between my mind and the discourse on fire-arms to which my friend treated me. We drank draught lager ; iced to an agreeable temperature.

After luncheon I was shown around the hotel ; all its wretched modern improvements were pointed out to me. I had to observe all the latest labour-saving devices. It was expected of me to comment blithely on the beautiful decorations. After a luncheon, too ! But I scored one off my professor of lethal weapons, by asking him if he had ever seen anyone " bumped off " by gangsters using a " Tommy-gun." He replied, " No." " Well, I have," says I. " Indeed ? " says he. " And where might that have been ? " " In your own city of New York ! " says I.

Thereafter, we no longer encroached on each other's business preserves, but over some really drinkable

coffee in the modern lounge, discussed the inertia of
the League of Nations.

For your amusement, here is a dinner menu from the
Strand Palace Hotel.

Les Huîtres sur Glacé.
Hors-d'Œuvre Variés.
Saumon Fumé.
Caviar Sévéruga.
Grape Fruit Cerisette.

———

Clear Mock-Turtle.
Crème Reine Perlée.

———

Blanc de Turbotin Héloïse
or
Feuilleté de Fruits de Mer.

———

Tournedos Chasseur.
Cœurs de Céleris à la Moëlle.
Pommes Croquantes.

———

Poularde en Cocotte Mascotte.
Salade Gauloise.

———

Bombe Glacée Tutti-Frutti.
Gaufrette.

Whilst I quibble at the accent on " glacé " I can
find no fault with this dinner as being a well-balanced
meal. If it is cooked and served as well as was the
luncheon I had, then it is to be recommended without
reserve.

I must make confession to having nursed a wrong impression of this hotel for many years. Apart from the fact that the foyer is slightly reminiscent of the railway station ebb and flow of humanity, the Strand Palace is definitely of a high order now. It is completely modernized—and if you don't believe that, express your doubt to one of the desk clerks ; before you know where you are, you'll be whisked away on a whirlwind tour of the hotel—you'll balance half-crowns on edge on the base of the dynamos, proving how vibrationless is the generating plant—you'll write letters frantically on every floor for the fun of posting them in the letter chute. You'll do many of these things maybe, but you'll never again call to question the modernity of the Strand Palace Hotel.

If you are wise, you'll profit by my experience—and just accept my statement as being fact.

P.S. Did you know that the ordinary Lyons tea-shop in Ludgate Circus is open all night ? Big-hearted Lyons—catering to the needs of thirsty newspaper workers ; thirsty, because the pubs are not open at night.

ROYAL PALACE HOTEL, *Kensington*.

This is the most exclusive and most expensive of all the hotels operated by—how did you guess it ?—J. Lyons & Co., Ltd.

The menus are in French and nothing else, so far as the Lucullus Restaurant is concerned. The Grill Room is more plebeian ; a great deal of the menu is in English and they even have a hot joint of "Boiled Gammon and Cabbage—1s. 9d." The mixed grill at the Strand Palace costs 2s. 2d. At the Royal Palace it is 3s. 6d. That's what you pay for snob-value.

Iced coffee at Maison Lyons is fourpence a glass ; at the Royal Palace Hotel it costs you one shilling.

Actually, quite apart from the difference in prices, there's no sense in attempting a comparison between this hotel and other establishments of Lyons. For the Royal Palace is meant to be good, expensive, quiet and dignified. It combines the excellence of the Trocadero cuisine with the peacefulness of the Ritz at three o'clock on a Sunday afternoon.

It succeeds admirably.

In addition to the Grill Room and Lucullus Restaurant is the famous Empress Rooms. This, at one time, was the place for supper and dancing. Now, although there is a steady and faithful clientèle, it is no longer "smaht" to go to the Empress Rooms. It's so far West of Piccadilly Circus as to be well-nigh provincial ; or suburban, which is worse.

This Lucullus Restaurant is an admirable place to take that finicky aunt of yours—especially if you have "expectations." You can be sure of a superb luncheon which should guarantee you the lifelong charge of the favourite canary in the old lady's Will.

Incidentally, what the chef here does not know about Homard Cardinal is nobody's business ! Even if it costs 8s. 6d. for two, it is well worth the price. So is the Porterhouse Steak at 9s. for two. But then, I have a spiritual affinity with all Porterhouse Steaks.

    *   *   *   *   *

Did you know that Lyons sell over two and a half million portions of ice-cream daily ?

REGAL CINEMA, *Marble Arch, W.1.*

No doubt you go to the Regal Cinema at Marble Arch. Should you do so without first consulting the critiques of C——c B——e in the D——y E——s, you are liable to strike a dud programme. Especially if you indulge in the habit of " dropping in " at cinemas.

But don't be downhearted if the movie happens to bore you to tears ; disregard the precise unemotionalism of Emmanuel Starkey and his Twelve Regal Virtuosi. Though it may be raining cats and dogs outside there is no need for you to leave the hospitable shelter of the building.

Upstairs in the foyer you can indulge your dancing propensities to the full at a Thé Dansant. How thoughtful of the Regal management. Should your partner be of the Dumb Dora type whose conversational abilities are considerably inferior to her physical

228

charms and her dancing prowess, you can pass the leisure moments in gazing at the " magnificent view of Hyde Park." The management boasts of this view ; for all the world as though it had been contrived for the especial benefit of Regal patrons.

So there you are ! You can see the picture—dance—and look at a view of Hyde Park ; all from this one cinema. No other movie house can lay claim to such distinction.

Elsewhere in this book I have touched lightly as a butterfly upon the claims for your notice set forward by Denman Street. To particularize somewhat, after paying another visit to that thoroughfare.

The *Marie Elizabeth Waffle Bar* specializes in two things. The first and least important is waffles. The second and most important is the pretty girls who serve you. Of their kinds, each of these is the best obtainable in London : so says Mr. Kahn who is the proprietor here. He works hard and long so that everything at his place shall be " just so." The result is, excellent waffles with the real thing in maple syrup served by highly efficient waitresses who do not spoil the view.

At *Abrahamson's* you can get " Gefülle Fische."

The Troika has a swinging signboard on which is a pretty picture of fur-hatted ruffians driving a three-horse sleigh. This means of transportation, so one is

informed, is a troika. The restaurant serves caviar
sandwiches at one shilling each, and caviar omelettes at
two shillings and fourpence. Now, caviar and hot egg
do not mix ; I will not believe that any intelligent
Russian ever ate a caviar omelette. So, I am forced to
deduce that this extraordinary dish was invented in
Denman Street by the Troika Restaurant. Caviar
omelette, forsooth !

Mrs. Cook's. Advertises outside " really nice omelettes." Don't be deterred by this " baby talk " advertising, for Mrs. Cook does not do her handiwork
justice by saying " really nice omelettes." They are
superb—and so cheap.

*   *   *   *   *

There are many recognized manufacturers of chocolates. Without hesitation, I award the palm of
excellence to *MM. Charbonnel and Walker Ltd.*, of 31,
*Old Bond Street, W.*1. They issue a list of over one
hundred varieties of chocolates ; describing each one
and numbering it. So you can choose the flavour
you want with the greatest of ease. Doesn't " Orgak "
appeal to you ? It's chocolate paste confected with
Orange Peel and Arak. The number is 29. Nougat,
vanille (petite) is No. 69. It's rather like studying
an ABC time-table—for there are signs against each
species of chocolate to denote whether it has a hard
or semi-hard interior ; whether it is specialized by
Charbonnel's.

Take it from me, however, a box of chocolates from this firm comprising the favourite kinds of the prospective recipient, is sure to please. I know. For, buying a large box here, I had it filled with what I thought would please a Certain Someone—and discovered I had chosen all my pet flavours. Well, what was one to do? Quite right. I ate the whole lot myself.

* * * * *

On the left-hand side of Regent Street, just beyond Swan & Edgar's is an inconsiderable arcade called Whirlwind Arcade. A doorway opens into the most Oriental café you could imagine after reading Sax Rohmer and seeing *Chu Chin Chow*. This is a place where you can get thimblesful of Turkish coffee; if you care for that nauseous, scented mud. It amazes me that the Turk drinks such stuff; for in other ways he shows a fine sense of discrimination and applied intelligence—those periodic massacres of Armenians. . . .

* * * * *

The *Trust Houses, Ltd.*, is an instance where the "chain system" of service to the public brings about good. About one hundred and eighty country hotels throughout the length and breadth of Great Britain have come under the Trust House management. They have been overhauled, renovated and licked into shape by the organization having its head-quarters in the slums of Covent Garden. Now, the motorist can get a three-course luncheon at any Trust House for half a crown, or a three-course dinner for three shillings or three-and-six.

If you stay *en pension* at one of these places, you can get a coupon from the reception office to entitle you to have luncheon at another Trust House. Thus, you are not bound to the same town for your midday grub ; but I'll bet you dollars to doughnuts there'll be very little difference in the actual food you get. Trust Houses, Ltd., stand for co-operation and standardization.

*   *   *   *   *

There is one famous place in London for " nut-fooders " and super-vegetarians. Many people know it : many visitors to this city would like to hear of its whereabouts. Close to the Alhambra is the restaurant of *Eustace Miles of Chandos Street*. He caters to your needs with synthetic cutlets of nuts ; synthetic steaks of bananas ; yet it is strange how these synthetic, meatless dishes have an eye-appeal, inasmuch as they are made to look similar to chops and steaks. That large numbers of people are vegetarians, and that this restaurant caters well to their wants, can be deduced from the difficulty of getting a seat in the Eustace Miles restaurant at meal-times.

*   *   *   *   *

Fleet Street offers more than Anderton's, The Cheshire Cheese and others that I have mentioned.

There is *Jolly's* for sandwiches.

Mooney's for Irish whiskey—it has an " e " in it, as well as a smoky flavour. Both are redundant, I think.

Peele's at 178, *Fleet Street*, is nearly opposite the Cock Tavern which is nearly opposite Peele's, which is . . . and that is all I'll say of those two.

Groom's Rainbow Tavern is under Bodega management.

The *Wig and Pen* is a tea-shoppie.

Best of all is the new *Daily Express* building.

* * * * *

S.P.O., *Waterloo Road, S.E.1.*

Under the railway bridge that spans the busy thoroughfare of Waterloo Road, is an eating-place trading under the cabalistic sign of S.P.O. It is a slightly more refeened version of Ted Shacklady's, of which I wrote earlier in this book.

S.P.O. has a deal of white tiling both inside and out, which helps to give an appearance of cleanliness. The menu is somewhat more varied than that of Ted Shacklady. You can get chops here, if you like to pay rather higher prices for a chop than Lyons charge you. Which does not seem right. For S.P.O. is dingy, whilst Lyons' places are all a-glitter. Other dishes, such as " eggs on chips," sausage and mashed, are all cheap. Tea or coffee costs you a mere tuppence a cup.

This place does a thriving business. For in the

neighbourhood are many warehouses, factories and the railway terminus of Waterloo. There is the Union Jack Club a scant hundred yards distant; hospitals who have large staffs, and finally, the Old Vic Theatre.

In mentioning the Old Vic, I would not suggest that the scene-shifters are patrons of S.P.O. Well, they may be, though I know it not. Of one thing I can be certain, however. Actors and actresses are staunch habitués of this little place; especially on Wednesdays and Thursdays—those being the days on which funds are particularly low in the case of theatrical people.

Be it said, that you will find the players from the Old Vic eating at the S.P.O. on other days of the week. For, on the salaries paid to Shakespearean actors and actresses, it's generally either the S.P.O. or a Lyons; the former seems to offer better value in filling food for money.

" It is a stern indictment on the public taste for theatrical fare that those who so skilfully depict the comedies and tragedies of that master-craftsman, Will Shakespeare, should be compelled to accept such paltry remuneration, that they are unable, etc., etc." One has yet to meet with a Shakespearean company that pays salaries commensurate with the demands made on the players.

Still, after many hours of blathering and mouth-

foaming these " poor players that strut and fret " on
the stage of the draughty Old Vic Theatre, are entitled
to eat. Go gaze your fill of these Thespians at the
S.P.O. Even in such a cheap place as this, these underpaid enthusiasts of the play have to consider well the
price of things before they order.

S.P.O. ? Sausages, potatoes and onions—one and
tuppence.

*   *   *   *   *

In Wardour Street, at the corner of Gerrard Street,
is *Maxim's Chinese Café*. You can have tea and dance ;
dinner and dance ; supper and dance. You can
have a special table d'hôte luncheon at two shillings
only.

The music is purveyed by a band of musicians representative of many nations ; of which China is the least
conspicuous.

The various managers, waiters and so on, look sus-
piciously at customers. So many brawls and riots have
taken place in Maxim's, that the staff is permanently
on the *qui vive* for trouble. Which is uncomfortable
for would-be well-behaved patrons.

The tense atmosphere has aroused in many otherwise
well-behaved people an insane longing to hurl plates
at the band, and follow up that performance with a
Red Indian war dance and scalping expedition.

Don't go to Maxim's for Chinese food, nor yet for
English dishes. The chefs have become dispirited

235

with trying to cook first one and then the other, and
have compromised by producing the inimitable cuisine
for which Maxim's is famous.

*   *   *   *   *

Yet should the urge to eat Chow Mein or any of the
various Chop Sueys be strong upon you, there is a
perfectly good *Chinese Café* in *Sherwood Street*. The
entrance is in Piccadilly Circus and you go upstairs.
All Chinese restaurants, the world over apparently,
involve either going upstairs or going downstairs.

If you are lucky enough to get a table by the window you can divert your mind from the weird dishes,
by watching the traffic gyrate around our old friend
Eros.

But your luncheon will be spoilt completely if some
one of your party begins an audible speculation as to
the fate of little dogs that meet their Waterloo at the
Battersea Dogs' Home. My luncheon was ruined ;
for I could almost see small tails wagging in the
conglomerate mass that was set before me.

On the menu, every dish is named in English and
Chinese ; there is a description of each—likewise a
number, by which you order. You can eat yourself to
a standstill for three shillings and sixpence, for the
portions are deceptively large ; thanks to the ubiquitous bowl of rice. All the sweets are too strange
for Western palates in my opinion.

The absurd tea-drinking ritual obtains. Which is

grotesque and out of place anywhere save in a tea-
garden east of Singapore.

Anyway, me no likee chop suey.

LE PERROQUET, 43, *Leicester Square*, W.1.

On the south-west corner of Leicester Square stands
a restaurant. For years, this particular corner has
been a shrine of mine. Once, when it was Restaurant
Boulestin under the flag of the one and only Mons.
X. M. Boulestin ; then, when the premises changed
hands and the restaurant was known as Maison Doré
I again was a patron—partly also to see Jimmy, the
maître d'hôtel, who was somewhat of a magician with the
chafing-dish. It had been my hope to include Maison
Doré in this book for three reasons. The first being
Jimmy ; the second, the perfect cuisine ; the third,
the wine cellars, which were unequalled in the whole
of London.

Alas ! As I took my sedate way on pilgrimage to the
place, I saw that it existed no more as a restaurant.
It was in the hands of builders and decorators.
Another pet place gone. Maison Doré was numbered
among the departed.

" Have you been to Le Perroquet ? " some one asked
me on the phone.

" Certainly not," I replied. " I don't like sandwich
bars. You ought to know that."

" It's not a sandwich bar. It's in . . ."

" . . . Soho," I finished. "Thanks very much. But I have been to Soho, in case you don't know."

"Don't be feeble-minded!" was the plea from the voice on the telephone. "Le Perroquet is where Maison Doré used to be!"

That conversation took place after breakfast. At lunch-time I was sitting in Le Perroquet. The same old premises : small, cosy and *intime*, but having undergone such a transformation. The colour scheme is in three shades of pink. You like it or you don't ; and if you don't, it doesn't matter really, for the blending of the pinks is calculated not to distract the attention from the pleasures of the table.

Here was another surprise! Le Perroquet is operated by none other than G. Bellometti, who is known to more people than seems possible.

"Bellometti? Sure I know the guy! Hell of a swell feller!"

"Der Herr Bellometti? Ja, freilich!"

"Monsieur Bellometti? Mais parfaitement ; il est le prince des restaurateurs!"

"Signor Bellometti? Ma che! Naturalimente!"

And here he is now—in spite of the restaurant in Soho trading under his name. Le Perroquet is his own place.

One basks, expands, grows amiable in the light of his pleasant, soothing personality—that is, if one happens to feel grouchy.

His secret? None other than that the details are

under his supervision. If you are without toast, he will bring it to you himself, before either you or a quick waiter are aware of the toast-shortage.

That's a big thing : the personal attention which is a sure way to success in the restaurant business.

There is a table d'hôte luncheon at five shillings and sixpence and a table d'hôte dinner at three shillings more. Both are excellent and offer a wide variety of choice. If there's nothing you want from either, you can eat table d'hôte—within limits, of course—from the à la carte menu.

Take my advice, however, and have Signor Bellometti choose you a table d'hôte luncheon. It's simple, and is sure to be perfect. As an example, I'll give you the menu of the luncheon I had. Yes ; I fell for table d'hôte ! I've starred my own choices.

Hors-d'Œuvre de Choix.
(*) Melon cocktail.
Crevettes.

(*) Raie au Beurre Noir
ou
Omelette Perroquet.

Côte de Veau Sautée Chasseur
ou
(*) Buffet Froid.

Haricots verts au Beurre.
Pommes à la Menthe.

(*) Entremet Maison.

From the cold buffet I chose Suprême de volaille glacé
and with it, young, green salad. And York ham, too !
As a sweet, I had strawberries and cream.

Now all that was perfectly cooked and served and
there was nothing stingy about the portions. A little
more of this ? Just a bit of that ? seemed to be the
song of the smiling waiters.

At five shillings and sixpence a luncheon such as
that cannot be surpassed. I shall repeat the performance, most certainly.

For your edification, here is a typical menu of the
eight-and-sixpenny dinner.

Hors-d'Œuvre Norvégienne.
Melon cocktail.
Crevettes.

———

Consommé Royal Printanière.
Crème Malakoff.

———

Homard Newbourg.
Blanchailles Diablées.

———

Poulet de Grain Mascotte
ou
Selection de Buffet Froid.

———

Fêues à la Crème.
Pommes Cocotte.
Salade Romaine.

———

Fraises Romanoff.

As yet I have not dined Au Perroquet. Long before you read this, however, I shall have become an established customer. Mine will be one of those familiar faces of the place—blending in rather nicely with the three shades of pink in the decorations.

The Signor Bellometti will not ram champagne down your throat. He is too much of an artist in food and its concomitant drink to be guilty of such bad form.

" What shall I have to drink ? " say to him. He will choose the right thing to suit the meal, the weather, your mood and—by some strange process of divination—your pocket.

He gave me two of his special recipes which are so terse and ambiguous that it is wise to go to Le Perroquet to understand what they really mean.

Fillet of Sole Perroquet.
>   Fillet of Sole Poche in White Wine.
>   Light Lobster Sauce.
>   Basket of Caviar and Asparagus Tips.

Suprême de Volaille Perroquet.
>   A wing of chicken steamed in Port.
>   Foie Gras or Truffles.
>   Served in Glass Dish with Fonds Artichokes.

The first costs three shillings and sixpence, and the

chicken five shillings. I defy you to make them correctly in your own home from the recipes I've handed on to you. Signor Bellometti explained the brevity of his instructions by saying that he did not want to startle people by the number of ingredients used, or the time and care that have to be taken in making these dishes.

So go along to Le Perroquet. Who knows—but that you and I will elect to eat there at the same time and yet remain unaware of each other ? At least, you can do something for me ; convey my best wishes to the Signor Bellometti.

TRICITY RESTAURANT, *Savoy Hill, Strand,* *W.C.2.*

A very effective advertising medium to demonstrate the uses of electricity. At least, the deft handiwork of the bartenders savours of the electric as they minister to those who are being eclectic. The bar, however, is only one section of the Tricity. Somewhere on the premises are Showrooms, where you may gaze your fill of such delights as electric fires, cookers, lamps and other domestic, labour-saving devices. I've never yet been in the Showrooms ; nor am I likely to go there!

Then again, there is also a Cocktail Lounge. I know that part of Tricity. There is a Quick Lunch Counter,

M. Bieri gave me two recipes. Here they are, in the original French.

Délices de Sole Tricity.

Poche au vin blanc et jus de citron. Echalottes fines herbes au beurre. Reduire la cuisson. Ajoutant une cuiller Sauce Hollandaise. 1 cuiller à dessert de crème pruettée. Assaisonner sel et poivre. Champignons eminencé. Dessus les filets sole napper de cette sauce. Garnie pointes asperge et homard. Bordiere de Pomme duchesse et glacé.

Suprème Volaille Tricity (or Theodora).

Suprème volaille suer au beurre pendant 5 minutes, saupoudré echalotte : reduire au Brandy Sauce crème. Garnie fond artichaut p. parisienne points asperges. Lamer de truffles.

The first one costs two shillings and ninepence. The second five shillings.

If you like, you can be fanciful enough to have chicken cooked in a paper bag. The Tricity chef does that freakish dish to perfection.

Again, if you like sweetbreads with a piquant white sauce, there's no place where such an entrée is better cooked. Should you choose this latter, you must remember to ask that the sauce be made really piquant :

otherwise it will be served *a goût anglais,* which in such a sauce means insipidity.

I have been told that the table d'hôte dinner is a matter of some excellence.

Here is a specimen for you to consider.

Hors-d'Œuvre Variés.
Grape Fruit aux Liqueurs.
Saumon Fumé.   Caviar d'Astrakan.

———

Consommé Chaud ou Froid
ou
Crème Solferino.

———

Filet de Sole Doria
ou
Blanchailles Diablées.

———

Ris de Veau Braisé Financière
ou
Poulet en Casserole à l'Estragon.
Haricots Verts au Beurre.
Pommes Nouvelles Rissolées.

———

Coupe Glacée Printanière.
Mignardises.

It certainly reads well. Especially as the price is a beggarly five shillings and sixpence including dancing and cabaret.

So now don't be hesitant in giving the Tricity a good trial.

Remember the good advice given you about Fred ;

and get Monsieur Emil on to the subject of Berne and the Kornkeller there !

*   *   *   *   *

The *Grosvenor House* is spacious and elegant. The food and service all that they should be. It is expensive, but a good place for supper dancing, and rightly popular with an ever-growing coterie.

*   *   *   *   *

Then there is the *Berkeley* on *Piccadilly*. Famous for many things, such as an unvarying perfection of food and service. Yet so good is the Berkeley that they welcome you just as cordially though your luncheon order be no more than a baked potato and celery. The courtesy and consideration that have made the Berkeley so pre-eminent, are in great part due to Ferraro, that prince of *maîtres d'hôtel*.

*   *   *   *   *

Would that I might say much of *Ciro's,* for it is a delightful place with food and service that are of Ciro-standard. But what would be the use ? Ciro's is a club.

*   *   *   *   *

THE SAVOY, *Strand*, W.C.2.

There is in London one place which is unfailingly excellent in hotel, restaurant and grill-room arrangement. Of course : the Savoy.

Whether you are two for a cosy dinner and dance, a

party of four or forty, or whether you want to give a slap-up banquet for four hundred—the Savoy always meets the case.

To write of it as I should would almost become an autobiography.

In my cub days, I headed Savoy-wards. If I wanted to take a man to a business lunch—then the Savoy was the logical place. Should my partner be of the feminine persuasion, I would suggest the Savoy hastily—before she did !

It is London's most progressive place of entertainment. Most particularly am I addicted to the Savoy. If I ever should change my opinion, then it will be because something is wrong with me—not with the Savoy.

Don't think I'm alone in thus eulogizing this place. There must be hundreds and thousands who think the same as I do.

So it is absurd to tell you anything about it. Why should I ? Do you want to know that the rising floor in the restaurant took six months to build and cost £10,000 ? Of course not.

What I will do, however, is to give you two recipes. M. Latry, the chef, thinks the first one is the most beautiful dish in the whole world. I'm not sure that he isn't right, too !

Faisan Doré Savoy.

A pheasant is stuffed with fresh truffles and heart

248

of celery, and cooked slowly in a casserole with Devonshire butter ; a glass of port and a glass of cream are poured over it. A sprinkling of lemon juice just as it turns to gold makes it complete.

The trouble about this way of doing pheasant is that once you have had it, no other method of serving that bird seems worth while.

Here is the other recipe.

Poire Commis Ginette.

A beautiful commis pear is first cooked in vanilla syrup, cooled, and then cut in half and the interior filled with marrons glace. It is dressed on ice-cream and covered with chocolate sauce.

That is one of M. Latry's favourite sweets. Any time the *maître* plans for me to eat a meal comprising both those recipes, then I shall know I have attained Nirvana.

The Savoy is the place that never lets you down. If you want a grilled steak " rare but flared on both sides," that is exactly the way you will get your steak.

If you feel eccentric and order a haddock to be served on a triangle of poached eggs, you'll get just that dish.

Carroll Gibbons with his band is at the Savoy. Carroll is no mean exponent of the pianoforte ;

though the band as a whole strikes me as being too " heavy " and mechanical.

Certainly the Savoy is a good place. I'll break engagements any time to accept invitations to Savoy. Try me ; just try me !

TABLE

Places marked with an asterisk (*) indicate dancing

Name	Address	Nationality	Speciality
Abrahamson's Restaurant	Denman Street, W.1	Kosher	Gefülte Fische
Ace of Spades*	Kingston By-Pass, Surrey	British	
Aerodrome Hotel	Purley Way, Nr. Croydon	British	
Anderton's Hotel	Fleet Street, E.C.4	British	
Appendrodt's	Piccadilly Circus, W.1	German	Frankfürter garniert
Astoria Dance Salon *	Charing Cross Road, W.1	British	
Au Chat Noir	Old Compton Street, W.1	French	Coffee and ham rolls
Au Jardin des Gourmets	6, Greek Street, W.1	French	Excellent bourgeoise cuisine
Au Petit Riche	44, Old Compton Street, W.1	French	Tournedos Petit Riche
Au Petit Savoyard	35, Greek Street, W.1	French	Lobster salad
Barbellion	70, New Bond Street, W.1	French	Cakes
Basque	Dover Street, W.1	French	" Everything, sir ! "
Bellometti	27, Soho Square, W.1	Franco-Italian	Ris de Veau Marcel
Bentley's Oyster Bar	8, Swallow Street, W.1	British	Shellfish
Berkeley Hotel *	Piccadilly, W.1	Cosmopolitan	

Name	Address	Nationality	Speciality
Birch's Restaurant	39A, Old Broad Street, E.C.2	British	Turtle Soup
Blue Cockatoo	Cheyne Walk, S.W.3	British	
Bodega	Bedford Street, W.C.2	British	Beer
Boulestin	25, Southampton Street, W.C.2	French	Filets de sole Véron
Boulogne Restaurant	27, Gerrard Street, W.1	French	
Brasserie Universelle	Piccadilly Circus, W.1	Anglo-Teutonic	Lager beer and such
Brent Bridge Hotel *	Hendon, N.W.1	Anglo-Teutonic	
Brice Restaurant	17, Old Compton Street, W.1	French	
Bristol Grill	Cork Street, W.1	British	Chops and steaks
Mrs. Brown's Teashop	Wardour Street, W.1	British	
Burford Bridge Hotel *	Nr. Dorking, Surrey	British	
Cadogan Arms	Church Street, Chelsea, S.W.3	British	Alcoholic refreshments
Café Anglais *	20, Leicester Square, W.1	French	
Café de Paris *	Coventry Street, W.1	French	
Café Royal	68, Regent Street, W.1	French	Poulet en papier
Carlton Hotel*	Haymarket, S.W.1	Cosmopolitan	
Casserole Restaurant	Fulham Road, S.W.3	Russian	Caviar sandwiches

252

Name	Address	Nationality	Speciality
Cedar House	Ripley, Surrey	Olde Eng-lishe	
Chantecler Restaurant	56, Frith Street, W.1	French	
Charbonnel & Walker, Ltd.	31, Old Bond Street, W.1	Anglo-French	Chocolates
Chatham Grill	Jermyn Street, W.1	Franco-British	
Chelsea Grill	Flood Street, S.W.3	British	
Cheshire Cheese	Fleet Street, E.C.4	British	Steak and Kid-ney Pudding
Chesterfield Arms	Shepherd's Mar-ket, W.1	British	
Chinese Res-taurant	Sherwood Street, W.1	Chinese	
Ciro's *	Orange Street, S.W.1	Franco-British	Noisette d'agneau Sévignè
Clarendon Hotel	Hammersmith, W.8	British	
Clock House	Ripley, Surrey	British	
Cock Tavern	Fleet Street, E.C.4	British	Devonshire Pie
Commercio Restaurant	65, Frith Street, W.1	Italian	Fritto misto
Mrs. Cook's	Denman Street, W.1	British	Omelettes
Corti's	Old Compton Street, W.1	Italian	Scalopinno Milanaise
Coventry Res-taurant	7, Rupert Street, W.1	Franco-British	
De Hem's	Macclesfield Street, W.1	British	Oysters and Welsh Rarebits

Name	Address	Nationality	Speciality
Dieudonné Restaurant	79, St. Martin's Lane, W.C.2	French	
Le Diner Français	Old Compton Street, W.1	French	
Dorchester House *	Park Lane, W.1	Cosmopolitan	Ciernikis
Driver's	46, Glasshouse Street, W.1	British	Shellfish
Eats	14, Gerrard Street, W.1	British	Waffles and Coco-cola
Eiffel Tower Restaurant	Percy Street, W.1	Anglo-German	
Escargot Bienvenu	48, Greek Street, W.1	French	Snails and frogs' legs
Falstaff Restaurant	70, Fleet Street, E.C.4	British	Hot veal and ham pie
Fava Restaurant	13, Frith Street, W.1	Italian	"Un buon' piatto di macaron'."
Felbridge Hotel	East Grinstead, Sussex	British	
Finch's	190, Fulham Road, S.W.10	British	Alcoholic beverages
First Avenue Hotel	High Holborn, W.C.2	British	
Florence Restaurant	53, Rupert Street, W.1	Anglo-French	Table d'hôte only
Frascati *	32, Oxford Street, W.1	French	Cœurs de Palmier
Fuller's, Ltd.	All over London	British	Walnut cakes
Gatti's	436, Strand, W.C.2	British	
Gennaro's Restaurant	63, New Compton Street	Italian	Trippa alla Genovese

Name	Address	Nationality	Speciality
Genova Restaurant	41, Whitcomb Street, W.1	Italian	
Gibb's Hatch	Cranleigh, Surrey	British	
Gilbert's Oyster Bar	3, Wardour Street, W.1	British	Shellfish
Gloucester Road Coffee Stall	Gloucester Road, S.W.7	British	Sandwiches
Gow's	357, Strand, W.C.2	British	
Groom's Rainbow Tavern	16, Fleet Street, E.C.4	British	
Grosvenor House *	Park Lane, W.1	Cosmopolitan	
Gunter's	72, New Bond Street, W.1	British	Ice cream and cakes
Hatchett's Restaurant	1, Dover Street, W.1	British	Lobster Delmonico
Holborn Restaurant *	218, High Holborn, W.C.1	British	
Honeydew	Strand, W.C.2	Anglo-Canadian	Honeydew drink
Hungaria *	14, Lower Regent Street, S.W.1	Hungarian	Paprika chicken
Isola Bella Restaurant	15, Frith Street, W.1	Italian	Entrecôte à la Planche
Ivy Restaurant	1, West Street, W.1	French	Sole Bonne Femme
Japanese Restaurant	New Compton Street, W.1	Japanese	Chopsticks—garnished
Jolly's	97, Fleet Street, E.C.4	British	Pies and sandwiches
Josef's	2, Greek Street, W.1	Serbian	Veal Goulasch

Name	Address	Nationality	Speciality
Kardomah	Piccadilly, W.1	British	Tea and coffee
Kensington Restaurant	Church Street, W.8	British	
Kettner's *	29, Church Street, W.1	French	Veal à la Stro-gonoff
King Lud	Ludgate Circus, E.C.4	British	Welsh Rarebits
Kit Cat *	Haymarket, S.W.1	Franco-British	
Les Lauriers Hotel	Jermyn Street, S.W.1	French	
Legrain's	Gerrard Street, W.1	French	Coffee
Lord Belgrave Hotel	Whitcombe Street, W.1	British	Steaks
J. Lyons & Co., Ltd. *	All over Britain	British	
Malmaison *	Stratton Street, W.1	French	
Manhattan Sandwich Bar	Shepherd's Market, W.1	British	Sandwiches
Marie Eliza-beth	Denman Street, W.1	British	Waffles
Mars	19, Frith Street, W.1	Italian	
Martinez Restaurant	Swallow Street, W.1	Spanish	Arroz à la Val-enciana
Maxim's *	Wardour Street, W.1	Chinese	
Mayfair Hotel*	Mayfair, W.1	Cosmopoli-tan	Volaille veille mode
Metropole Hotel *	Northumberland Avenue, S.W.1	Cosmopoli-tan	Fricassé de Vol-aille Capucine

Name	Address	Nationality	Speciality
Eustace Miles	40, Chandos Street, W.C.2	British	Vegetarian
Mitre Hotel	Hampton Court	British	Sherry
Monico	19, Shaftesbury Avenue, W.1	French	Perdreau Monico
Monseigneur *	Piccadilly, W.1	French	
Monte Carlo Restaurant	1, Leicester Street, W.1	French	
Mooney's Irish House	Fleet Street, E.C.4	Irish	Whiskey
Moulin d'Or	27, Church Street, W.1	French	
Museum Restaurant	High Holborn, W.C.1	Franco-Italian	
Oddenino's	54, Regent Street, W.1	French	
Old Barn	Hildenborough, Kent	British	
Old Bell Hotel	Hurley, Bucks	British	Week-ends
Oriental Café	Denman Street, W.1	Turkish	Pilaffs
Pagani's	42, Great Portland Street, W.1	Anglo-Italian	
Peele's	178, Fleet Street, E.C.4	British	Chops
Perroquet, Le	43, Leicester Square, W.1	French	Suprême de Volaille Perroquet
Piccadilly Hotel *	Piccadilly, W.1	Cosmopolitan	Veal cutlet " Bitter Sweet "
Pinoli's	17, Rupert Street, W.1	British	Table d'hôte
Pitt's Cottage	Westerham, Kent	British	Home-made cakes

Name	Address	Nationality	Speciality
Prompt Corner Restaurant	19, Rupert Street, W.1	British	Cheap table d'hôte
Punch Bowle	Crawley, Surrey	British	
Punch Bowle	Horsham, Sussex	British	
Queen's Restaurant	Sloane Square, S.W.3	British	
Quo Vadis Restaurant	27, Dean Street, W.1	Franco-Italian	Suprême de Volaille à la Délysia
Regal Cinema*	Marble Arch, W.1	British	
Regent Palace Hotel *	Piccadilly Circus, W.1	British	
Reggiori Restaurant	1, Euston Road, N.W.1	Italian	
Rendezvous Restaurant	45, Dean Street, W.1	Franco-Italian	
Ridgeway's	Piccadilly, W.1	British	Tea
Ritz Hotel *	Piccadilly, W.1	Cosmopolitan	Poularde Chevalier
Royal Palace Hotel *	Kensington, W.8	British	
Royal Trocadero Restaurant	81, New Oxford Street	Italian	
Rule's	Maiden Lane, W.C.2	British	Chops and things like that
Rumpelmayer	72, St. James's Street, S.W.1	French	Cakes
Sandy's	Oxendon Street, W.1	British	Sixty kinds of sandwiches
Savoy Hotel *	Strand, W.C.2	Cosmopolitan	Faisan Doré Savoy
Schmidt's	41, Charlotte Street, W.1	Teutonic	Pig's knuckles and sauerkraut

Name	Address	Nationality	Speciality
Scott's	18, Coventry Street, W.1	British	Fish
Selfridge's	Oxford Street, W.1	British	American dishes
S.F. Snack Bar	Denman Street, W.1	British	Snacks
Ted Shack-lady's	222, East India Dock Road, E.14	British	
Shafi Restaurant	18, Gerrard Street, W.1	Indian	Curries
Short's	333, Strand, W.C.2	British	Alcoholic beverages
Simpson's	100, Strand, W.C.2	British	Roast saddle of mutton
Six Bells	King's Road, Chelsea, S.W.3	British	Cheap table d'hôte
Skindle's Hotel *	Maidenhead	British	
Snow's	3, Sherwood Street, W.1	British	Chops and steaks
Spider's Web Restaurant	Watford By-Pass, Herts	British	
Hotel Splendide * (Grill Caucasien)	Piccadilly, W.1	Russian	Schaslich
S.P.O.	Waterloo Road, S.E.1	British	Sausages, potatoes, onions
Stewart's	Regent Street, W.1	British	Ice-cream sodas
Stone's	Panton Street, S.W.1	British	Steak and Kidney Pudding
Strand Palace Hotel *	Strand, W.C.2	British	

Name	Address	Nationality	Speciality
Sweeting's	159, Cheapside, E.C.2	British	Shellfish and grills
Talbot Hotel	Ripley, Surrey	British	
Taverna Medicea	45, Frith Street, W.1	Italian	Risotto con funghi
Tony's Restaurant	58, New Compton Street, W.1	Italian	Scallopino chez Tony
Treviglio	12, Church Street, W.1	Italian	
Tricity *	125, Strand, W.C.2	British	Suprême de Volaille Tricity
Trocadero Grill Room	Nr. Piccadilly Circus, W.1	Franco-British	Soufflé Glacé Marjorie
Troika Restaurant	Denman Street, W.1	Russian	Caviar Omelettes
Trust Houses	All over Britain	British	
Veerasawmy	Swallow Street, W.1	Indian	Curried chicken Madras
Hotel Victoria	Northumberland Avenue, W.C.2	Cosmopolitan	Noix de Ris de Veau Pecheresse
Villa Villa	37, Gerrard Street, W.1	Italian	Table d'hôte
Waldorf Hotel *	Aldwych, W.C.2	Cosmopolitan	
Watermill Restaurant *	Dorking, Surrey	British	
White Lion Hotel	Cobham, Surrey	British	
Wig and Pen Restaurant	Fleet Street, E.C.4	British	
World's End	Cobham, Surrey	British	Home cooking

INDEX

INDEX

INDEX

266

267

INDEX

INDEX

273

INDEX

Printed in Great Britain by Butler & Tanner Ltd., Frome and London
F50.133